# Terracotta Ovens of My Childhood

The Story of a Little Girl from a Small Town
Called Czernowitz: A Memoir

by

Elite Olshtain

DORRANCE PUBLISHING CO., INC.
PITTSBURGH, PENNSYLVANIA 15222

*All Rights Reserved*
Copyright © 2010 by Elite Olshtain
No part of this book may be reproduced or transmitted
in any form or by any means, electronic or mechanical,
including photocopying, recording, or by any information
storage and retrieval system without permission in
writing from the author.

ISBN: 978-1-4349-0653-3
Printed in the United States of America

*First Printing*

For information or to order additional books, please write:
Dorrance Publishing Co., Inc.
701 Smithfield St.
Pittsburgh, Pennsylvania 15222
U.S.A.
1-800-788-7654
*www.dorrancebookstore.com*

# Contents

1. Life is Good .................................................................1
2. The Russians Are Coming! ...............................................8
3. The Romanians Are Back and the Nazis Are Here with Them! .......................................................................14
4. Living with Baba ..........................................................27
5. Life at Tante Rosa's......................................................36
6. The Yellow Star of David ..............................................44
7. We Are Back at Our Apartment ....................................50
8. The Russians Are Here Again! ......................................55
9. Frieda ........................................................................59
10. Willy..........................................................................69
11. My Father's Great Disappointment ..............................80
12. Learning to Play with Children My Age .......................85

13. Leaving Czernowitz..........................................................89
14. Can We Be a Family Again? ............................................94
15. The First Day of School...................................................97
16. Life Under the Communists .........................................105
17. A Long Journey to a New Country..............................112
18. A New Beginning..........................................................116
19. Becoming a Sabra.........................................................124
20. Epilogue – visiting Czernowitz 60 years later (2006)..133

# Preface

For years I did not want to tell my story. I had survived the Holocaust, and so did many others, but my story was—nothing! I was all right, and my family, by some miracle, was also all right. What was there to tell? This was a simple story of survival in bad times, but I never really had to look death in the face, and I did not see other people being killed, I only heard about it. How could my story compare to the terrible things people told about during fifty years following the war?

I felt guilty to even mention the fact that I was a Holocaust survivor, and I really did not want anyone to know about it. I tried to pretend I was a *sabra* (Israeli-born) and had a normal childhood like any other child in my class or in my surroundings. I did not want to remind myself, but I remembered. I remembered in very clear and precise pictures all the events I lived through. People used to say to me, "One cannot remember anything from the age of four or less." I listened, but I knew that I remembered things from when I was two and two and a half. These were only pictures through the eyes of a child, but they were vivid and clear, and no one else knew about them.

Then one day I saw the movie "Hope and Glory" and decided that even a story that is not tragic can be important, when told through the memories of a child. I decided that perhaps I *had* a story to tell. Still, I could not tell it as long as my mother and father were alive. It might have been too painful for them and impossible for me to tell the whole truth. My relations with my parents had always been complicated, and I felt that they could not withstand the book that I intended to write.

I also felt I needed to do some research and find out whether the things I remembered had any relationship to the actual historical events. Orly, the youngest of my three daughters, dedicated herself to the task of researching the events related to the story in this book. We were constantly surprised by the perfect match between some childish memories and the actual facts. So here it is—the way I remember it, the way a little girl saw the war events through personal vision.

# Chapter One

# Life Is Good

I was born on March 26, 1938, in the lovely town of Czernowitz. Spring was showing its first signs, and the streets were a mixture of snow and slush. Inside the two-room flat, on the second floor of a modern apartment building on Franzensgasse, it was warm. A fire was burning bright in the large brown terracotta oven.

Dr. Segal delivered me early in the morning of March the twenty-sixth after he and his wife had spent the evening playing cards with my parents and enjoying the famous *fluden* (crispy nut cake) that my grandmother used to bake. The Segals were Jewish neighbors who lived one floor above us. Both couples, like most of the other tenants, belonged to the upper middle class in Czernowitz. These were young people who had managed to reach a comfortable way of life and had plans for the future.

As usual, the conversation during that evening focused on the state of the troubled world. My mother, Frieda, who was the practical realist in the group, claimed that basically life for the Jews in Czernowitz was better than anywhere else in the world. Despite the Romanian hooligans who made the streets unsafe for Jews at night and in spite of the growing anti-Semitism, life was good. Yet secretly my mother had made her plans to immigrate to America if the situation deteriorated.

My father, Willy (short for Willhelm, was the idealist of the group. He had been greatly influenced by the recent visit of my mother's brother, Tarzan (Srul), who was living at the time on a kibbutz in Palestine. Srul (the Yiddish version of Israel) had spent a year in Czernowitz as a *shaliach* (Zionist delegate) from Palestine. Everybody called him Tarzan because he resembled the actor playing Tarzan in the movies of those days. He was a true socialist, with unusual charisma and enthusiasm. My father's three brothers and Srul, my mother's oldest brother, had all immigrated to Palestine ten years earlier as devout members of the Shomer Hatzair movement (a socialist youth movement). In Palestine they had participated in building new kibbutzim (communal farms).

My father was the only member of his family who remained in Czernowitz. He had stayed behind to continue the family's marble business, as he had promised his father on his deathbed. This was a business that had been passed on from generation to generation, and Willy was in charge of it now.

So my father, in that slightly detached manner of his, spoke of Palestine and the opportunity to build a new and just society in their ancestral land. His words sounded romantic and so far away from Hitler's atrocities against the Jews in Germany and Austria. My mother was quick to remind everybody at the table that Palestine was a hard and arid land. The Jews there were poor and had to struggle and break their backs in hard physical labor for a dream that may never come true. She too mentioned her brother but in the context of a promising young man who had given up everything good in his life: the chance to study medicine in Vienna, to marry a rich woman, and to become an important member of the Jewish community in Czernowitz. For what? Malaria and a meager existence on a commune in a desert land, with a quiet and reserved wife who was far below what her wonderful brother deserved. Granted they had a beautiful son, but he could not speak a word of German, so what education might he pursue in his life? No, if she had to leave Czernowitz it would only be for America. There they could build a new life in the free world.

Dr. Segal was the pessimist in the group. He had no plans to leave Czernowitz even though he could visualize a crazed Hitler taking over the world and making life for the Jews unbearable even here in Bukovina, (the district to which Czernowitz belonged), where Jews had lived relatively comfortably until now. It appeared that Carol, the Romanian king, was on very good terms with the Germans. So the future looked very precarious to Dr. Segal.

Mrs. Segal was a quiet woman who did not speak much. Having come from a poor family, she felt blessed to be married to a successful obstetrician and to be living in the center of town in an apartment with electricity, running water, and all the comforts of the time. From time to time she would almost whisper to herself: "We finally have a good life here. I am not going to give this up. Hitler won't stay in power forever, and anyway he is far away from us. Czernowitz has always been a Jewish town. Can you imagine this town without Jews? We need to stay and make the best we can, right here." So the discussion ended that night with everyone smiling and longing to join her in her optimism.

My parents got married in Czernowitz in 1935. My mother came from a poor and simple family, the Furmans, who lived in the poorest part of town. My father came from an upper middle class family with a well-established business in the center of the *Russischen Gasse*. His father owned a marble workshop and had done very well during the Austro-Hungarian period prior to the First World War and continued to do well by getting jobs from the municipality during the Romanian period. In the beginning of the twentieth century the firm had been commissioned to do the façade of the new theatre. This was a very important commission since the theatre came to be recognized as an architectural jewel in that part of the world. From then on, the Zellers were recognized as one of the best marble establishments in town, next to just one other firm, the Moscaliuks.

Shortly after my parents got married in the spring of 1936, my grandfather, Simcha, had a heart attack, and on his deathbed he made my father promise that he wouldn't leave Czernowitz and would continue to run the family business. *We have proven that our Jewish craftsmanship is just as good as the famous Moscaliuks. Let us make sure that we continue this tradition.*

My father's mother, Sara, left right after her husband's death and joined her other three sons in Palestine. Although she had always been a very observant, religious woman, she went to live on a Hashomer Hatzair kibbutz, which was entirely non-observant. At first she was shocked and greatly distressed, but after talking to her rabbi in town, she established a religious-kosher corner in the large kibbutz kitchen where she cooked for all the elders on the kibbutz. This became to be known as the first kosher corner in a kibbutz kitchen.

My father was now the only Zeller in Czernowitz, and he ran a very efficient marble business. Most of his work centered on making granite tombstones for the Jewish Cemetery. He regarded his work as a special Jewish art, which had been passed on to him from his ancestors. He was very skilled and could produce beautiful engraved letters both in Hebrew and German. A large granite tombstone that left his workshop was considered a unique creation and a work of art. He took great pride in his work and usually signed his name, Willhelm Zeller, at the bottom of the tombstone.

Both my parents had been active in Hashomer Hatzair as youngsters. They often met at Zionist speeches delivered at the Jewish Cultural Center, an impressive building near the theatre. There they heard speakers such as Usishkin, Sokolov, and Jabotinsky. They both spoke Hebrew quite well but were not very devoted Zionists and were more concerned with furthering their own careers and well-being. My father had studied briefly in

Vienna in 1929-1930, and my mother had received a teacher's certificate from the famous Safra Ivria in Czernowitz. Soon after they got married they purchased the apartment on Franzensgasse, in a newly built Bau Haus building, and my mother became a full and active partner in the marble-business. She had a natural flare for business and soon learned to make contacts with all the important municipal agencies and building companies, and the business was flourishing.

When the date of my birth was getting near, my mother, like many middle class Jewish women, made arrangements to get a German nanny to take care of me. She had no intention of staying home and wanted to continue her work in the business. So after a few interviews she found the perfect nanny—a young woman named Erica, who spoke impeccable German and always wore a *dirndl (*the Austrian national dress).

The apartment on Franzensgasse was not large, but it was comfortable. There was a large living room with three large windows overlooking the street. The furniture in it was modern and comfortable, and my parents even owned a radio and a large piano. The bedroom was the second large room with a small porch to the backyard. Both rooms had large terracotta ovens, which required quite a lot of wood for heating in the winter.

The kitchen had a huge oven in it and a large table for the whole family to eat at. From the kitchen there was one door to a maid or nanny's room and another door to a storeroom. But most importantly, there was a separate toilet with running water like in any modern building. In the late thirties, anyone who owned such an apartment in the center of town was doing all right, and my mother was very proud of it.

On the morning I was born, my maternal grandmother, Sabina, was summoned to help. She was a very wise and practical woman who immediately took care of things. Erica was to start working a few days later, and everything had to be set up so that she would be comfortable in her little room and I would have all the equipment a baby could have in those days. My grandma, Sabina (or Sima as she was often called), and my dad took care of everything while my mother stayed in bed for a whole week just nursing me and resting. Dr. Segal would not let her leave the bed for at least ten days, but he gave in after a week since she was strong and active and wanted to return to her regular activities.

My grandma was excited and happy and kept dancing with me in her arms. "This little girl will have a good life. She has been born into comfort from the start, not like her mother who was born just a year before the big war. She will never have to suffer through a war like the one we had to live through." Little did she know!

Erica was a very proper young woman: very polite, super clean, and with a strict German upbringing. She gave me a very meticulous bath every morning, dressed me up in the most beautiful baby clothes, and put me in the stroller to take me to my mother at the business where she would nurse me and then go on with her work. Twice a day Erica went back and forth with me in the stroller. Luckily the first months of my life were spring and then summer, a wonderful time to walk along the streets of Czernowitz.

Erica fell in love with me the first moment she saw me and treated me royally all along. "Isn't this an aristocratic looking baby?" she used to say to friends or neighbors she met on the street. "She will surely grow up to be a very fine lady." Erica's whole focus in life at the time was to bring me up as a very privileged little girl.

The bad news from Germany kept coming one after the other. In April of 1938 the last of the Jewish businesses were closed and all Jewish shops were transferred to Germans. In July Jewish physicians were banned and Jewish pupils were expelled from schools. Jews could not use German names and had to add a middle name—Israel for males and Sara for females. On Yom Kippur of 1938, the prominent rabbi Leo Baek of Berlin said, in front of his congregation, "We shall bow before God but remain standing before man." Still the Jews in Czernowitz continued leading their normal lives hoping that the nightmare would soon end—it had to, the German people would not let it continue.

Yet nobody seemed to stop the atrocities. It was as if the world accepted the Nazi regime as a necessary evil, and since most people thought that the Jews deserved some restrictions, no one really interfered with Germany. And then came the terrible *Kristallnacht* in November 1938, just as I was beginning to make my first childish sounds, crawling rapidly through the big apartment and smiling happily at everyone.

The "Crystal Night" shocked everybody. Erica heard about it too. She had always been proud to work for a young Jewish couple in the center of Czernowitz, but suddenly she became a little suspicious. She continued to do her job efficiently and properly, and she loved me dearly, as always, but there was a slight uneasy feeling in the air.

My mother got into a real frenzy after the Crystal Night. Once a week she went for a whole day to the small villages and communities around Czernowitz where she bought Romanian embroidered blouses, nightgowns, and tablecloths. She packed them into neat little packages and sent them off to my father's sister in Los Angeles. Week after week she carried the small packages to the post office. In the evening she told my father "Don't worry; we will soon have a lot of money at your sister's in America. She is a bright woman; she will sell the embroidered stuff. I hear Americans love handmade things. Then one day she will be able to send us the affidavit, and we will leave this place forever and make a new life for ourselves in America." My father listened to her but said nothing; he kept thinking of the promise he made his father, *never to leave Czernowitz.*

My parents loved to discuss the day's events just before they fell asleep, and every night the thought of America gave them the courage to go on and continue living their comfortable life in Czernowitz.

# Chapter Two

# The Russians Are Coming!

On June the twenty-eighth of 1940, a bright summer morning, being just a little over the age of two, I woke up in my little bed in the living room and was surprised that everything was very quiet. The sun was filling the whole living room, and everything seemed so bright and neat, but there were no sounds to be heard. The street was quiet; the house was quiet. Where was Erica? She had suddenly disappeared from my life. I was sitting in my bed and listening to the silence.

Suddenly both my parents walked into the living room. They had big smiles on their faces, and they seemed happy. My father took me out of my bed and brought me into the kitchen. He had prepared my breakfast. What was happening? How come both of them were home and had time for me?

After breakfast they sat down at the table in the living room with some notes and books and began singing in a strange language. I wanted to join in, so they taught me some of these strange words, which were so different from the German words I knew. "*Maguchaya, Kipuchaya…*" We were all sitting together and singing happily in Russian.

In June of 1940—a particularly hot summer in Czernowitz—the Russians took over. This followed the infamous agreement between Riventrop and Molotov, by which Germany and the USSR agreed to divide Poland between them, and the USSR also received control over the territories of North Bukovina and Bessarabia. Thus Czernowitz became an important center for the Russian occupation.

The Jews, who had suffered from the anti-Semitic Romanian governments, were hoping that the Russians would be better. The first few days were very quiet; people stayed home and waited to see what would happen.

In our apartment we were a family of three: my father, my mother, and me. My devoted nanny, Erica, had left a few weeks earlier. She came to my parents and said that she had to leave right away to go take care of an old aunt who was dying somewhere in Hungary. She disappeared, and we never heard from her again. For my mother this meant that she could not go to work as regularly as she wanted, but my grandmother, Sabina, would come and help.

When the Russians entered Czernowitz everything seemed very peaceful and relaxed, at least through the eyes of a two-year-old. My parents stayed home and stopped going to their business. Their competitor, the famous Moscaliuk, had disappeared, and his business looked deserted. It was not a good idea to have a prospering business in the communist world, and so my parents closed down their business, pulled down the sign bearing the name of Zeller, and just enjoyed being home with me. The socialist ideals that both of them knew well, but particularly my father also believed in, were rekindled by the idea that they were now part of the USSR. They decided right away to learn Russian, and my father went out for a few hours and returned with a lot of books in Russian and some teaching materials.

We used to sit for hours at the table in the living room and practice sentences in Russian and sing a lot of songs in Russian.

I too learned to sing some songs in my childish voice and developing speech, and some of the words I still remember. My father had a beautiful voice, and he taught me to imitate the Russian words.

It seemed a quiet and calm life, although things were particularly bad for two groups of Jews: the communists who thought their good times had come but who were soon deported to Siberia as "dangerous" elements, and the Jewish bourgeois class, who were perceived as rich and decadent. Where did my parents belong? My father believed in the socialist-communist ideas and was eager to become involved in the new system. As a young student in Vienna he had been active in the socialist movement there. My mother, the practical one, thought that we needed to make a living and we had to be acceptable in the new society. She would soon have a brilliant idea.

As soon as the Russians came into Czernowitz they replaced all signs of Romanian rule with signs of communism. In the Ring Plaz they put up a huge picture of Stalin. They built a column with a Russian star on the top, and pictures of Lenin, Stalin, Marx, and Engels appeared everywhere. My parents looked, with some distaste, at the quickly drawn figures that sprang up everywhere, and my father began sketching some of them. He was very good with black and white sketches, which he did for his professional work designing marble facades or for personal enjoyment.

My mother went to the authorities and suggested that they employ my father as a *chudoznik* (artist painter) to make portraits of the important leaders such as Lenin, Stalin, and the others. She brought some of his sketches, and they were very impressed. "Good. Let him work for us, and we will give him paper and paints, as much as he needs." My father was now employed by the Russians, so for the time being things were good.

At work he met other people, and soon they discovered that he sang Russian songs quite beautifully. He was invited to parties of the important leaders in the town. For almost a year life was pretty good for us, except for the fact that my mother had to stay home with me a lot, and that did not make her too happy. Still under the circumstances we were doing all right.

The news from the war in Europe was not good. The Russians realized that they had to be ready for war and had to build a strong army.

All the young men in Czernowitz were gradually recruited to the Russian Red Army. Even Dr. Segal, who had been working at a hospital, was recruited, and so was my father. They all ended up in a training camp in Rosh, which was a large area of woods and open fields. The "Jewish Group" from Czernowitz was well known—many of them had been in youth movements and active in the Maccabiah so they were young, strong, and very supportive of each other. My father, *Tata* as I called him, was loved by all: He knew just a little Russian but sang a lot of beautiful songs in Russian, and his clear tenor brought tears to many eyes. Most of all, he was appreciated for his physical strength. Although he was not a tall man he was very strong. In fact my mother fell in love with him when she had watched him do his athletics at Maccabiah in Czernowitz. Also many Russian soldiers, who could not live without a daily portion of alcohol, loved him. Being a former Shomer Hatzair member he drank no alcohol, and so he was happy to give his ratio of vodka to a Ukrainian or Russian friend.

Once a week my mother and I would visit Tata. We would walk past the Schiller park, downhill to Rosh. He would wait for us at the bottom of the hill, stretching his arms to catch me. I would run down the whole hill to receive his hug. He was always so happy to see me! He would say to my mother in German, "She grew so much; she is so pretty; she speaks so beautifully!".

My father always had a little present ready for me, usually a piece of stone that he had carved into a little animal or a doll. He would take me into the woods and throw me in the air and play with me the whole time we were there for the visit. We sat under the apple trees and ate some *butter brot*, which we brought from home, and some apples from the trees. He often managed to tell me some stories and teach me some more Russian songs. Sometimes my mother would get a little annoyed with him for not giving her more time. She wanted to discuss the situation, the difficulties, the worries for the future, but he always said: "Frieda, we don't know what tomorrow will bring, so let us enjoy today."

After each visit at Rosh we would go home a little sad. I was sad because I did not want to say goodbye to Tata, and my mother was sad because her worries had not really been shared by my father. Sometimes we went directly home to our apartment on Franzensgasse, where we now lived, just the two of us. The apartment seemed very empty now, and we did not even use the bedroom. Instead we both slept in the living room near the radio. Other times we went to my grandmother's house, where we always got some good food. At the time I did not realize that it was very cheap food, such as cooked and mashed beans with sugar, spread on a slice of dark bread. To me it tasted delicious.

I loved my visits to my grandmother. My grandfather usually slept in his large bed and paid very little attention to us. My mother and my grandmother always had a lot to talk about, and I could play in the huge yard where the chickens and the geese were running around. There were also non-Jewish children who ran barefoot and played while pushing around large wheels. They were noisy and spoke a strange language (Romanian), which I had not heard in our house. But they were fun to watch.

My grandmother, Baba as I called her, had two tiny rooms in a little house, which was part of a whole complex of little houses built around a large yard. This complex was at the edge of the town above a huge green valley where the trains passed by. The neighbors went past each other's houses several times during the day, and everybody knew what was happening in everybody else's house. To me this was paradise—so lively and different from our clean, proper apartment in town. They all shared some crude field-toilets, which were holes dug in the ground and surrounded by a wooden structure. I did not have to use them since there was a potty in the house especially for me.

During our visits to Baba my mother would sit with her for hours at the kitchen table, and they would talk in low voices. Every time we came there my mother would bring a package from home, and Baba would put it in one of her little cupboards. The empty cupboards soon filled up with things we brought from our apartment: linen, tablecloths, silver cutlery, expensive clothes, furs, etc. I did not know why my mother did that, but I was happy to go there and I loved to stay with my grandmother when my mother went away on errands.

The days went by slowly, the faces of the grown-ups grew sadder and sadder as they listened to the news on the radio and told each other what they had heard. I, on the other hand, was happy to have some freedom in Baba's house and thrived on the visits to Rosh.

# Chapter Three

# The Romanians Are Back and the Nazis Are Here with Them!

A terrible sequence of explosions and loud sounds woke my mother and me up in the middle of the night. Every few seconds there was either a whistling sound or an explosion and the lights in our apartment went out. We had some candles, which my mother lit with trembling hands, and I kept quiet and did not dare to even breathe too loudly. I was a little over the age of three and clearly understood something bad was happening.

Suddenly we heard a loud knocking on the front door. Our neighbor Mrs. Segal stood there trembling with tears coming down her cheeks: "The German army has invaded Russia. Our husbands will be killed. What shall we do?"

In the meantime another neighbor came running down the stairs and said, "Just lock your apartment, and let's run across the street to the bomb shelter. Bombs are falling everywhere…"

My mother said nothing. She grabbed me in her arms, locked the apartment, and we ran down the stairs. We crossed the street, still running, and we saw a lot of other people running in the same direction. It was June and the morning was chilly but not really cold, and so my mother did not take any sweaters or blankets, but other people were carrying bundles with them. I thought to myself: *Why is everybody so frightened? What are bombs? I have to see what a bomb is!* So I looked up toward the sky, but all I could see were some flashing lights and tree branches falling down on us. For years to come I would imagine that a bomb is a big tree falling on you from the sky.

This was the last week in June 1941, when Germany invaded the Soviet Union and the Russians had to flee Czernowitz. The Russian army units stationed in Rosh, with my father, Dr. Segal, and many other young Jews from Czernowitz, were evacuated over night, and the Romanian and German troops took over Bukovina and of course Czernowitz. While exchanging hands, there were a few days of bombardment, but the takeover was swift and shocking.

When things quieted down a bit we went to Rosh to try to find out what happened to my father, but the Russians were gone and there were Romanian soldiers there. Romanian and German flags replaced the red flags. There was no one to talk to, and again we had to rely on rumors. My mother spoke to everyone she knew but could get no information.

During the following month we were going back and forth between our apartment and my Baba's house. I stayed with her more and more while my mother tried to get information about my father. Finally a Jewish soldier who had escaped the evacuation to Russia told the Czernowitz community that all the Jews who had been recruited to the Red Army were on the same train, which was heavily bombarded by the Germans, and they were all killed. He said that he was the only survivor from the "Jewish regiment." My mother came back to my baba's house with the news, but she said right away, "I don't believe Willy is dead. I am sure he escaped somehow, and we need to find a way to get in touch with him."

By that time, the Jewish community in Czernowitz had lost many of its members. At least 10,000 Jews had been deported to Siberia by the Soviets. Others were killed or ran away. Several thousand young people had been recruited to the Red Army. The Romanians and the Nazis killed about a thousand Jews within the first few days of their invasion in June 1941. Ukrainian hooligans roamed the city and robbed and looted many Jewish stores and homes. The Jews tried to stay indoors and keep as quiet as possible.

I was happy to stay with my grandmother, and I played most of the day in the big yard with the other kids. My baba always had something good for me to eat, although many Jewish families were suffering from lack of food. She had many friends among the Ukrainian villagers, and they would come by her house and sell her some butter, cheese, and bread, and so we managed quite well.

By the end of the summer my mother and I were staying at my grandmother's home and were not even visiting our apartment. I later understood that it had been confiscated by the Romanian army. Then one morning, on October eleventh, many Jews—women, men, children, and old people—started pouring into the big yard. My grandmother's neighborhood had become the Jewish ghetto.

Early in the morning of that October day, the leaders of the Jewish community were called to the office of the Romanian army governor of the town, General Vasily Ionescu. There, the governor issued instructions to establish a ghetto in the northern, lower part of town, where about 10,000 very low income Jews already lived (as well as many non-Jews). All the Jewish inhabitants of Czernowitz were to go there immediately, taking with them only the minimum belongings that they could carry. By the end of the day at 6:00 p.m., any Jew found outside the ghetto would be executed on the spot. During the day 40,000 Jews from all over town joined the 10,000 already there. At exactly 6:00 p.m. Romanian soldiers surrounded the ghetto, put up a temporary wooden fence all around it, and added barbed wire. Armed guards were placed at the entrances to the ghetto.

Baba's little house became a refuge place for many women. Some were cousins and aunts, and others were neighbors or strangers. Next to the large bed there were more beds and mattresses, and the whole house looked to me like a carpet of women. My grandfather, *Djadja* as I called him, was asked to sleep in the shed with other men.

The women had arrived in the ghetto wearing beautiful clothes, holding suitcases and bags. Their faces were sad, and they spoke very little. Some of my mother's cousins, who I remembered and who used to be so nice to me in the past, paid no attention to me now. Actually except for my grandmother, no one really noticed me, not even my mother. So no one told me what to do. I had a wonderful time running around, playing, singing, and standing near the fence of the ghetto and watching the Romanian soldiers march by through the cracks in the wooden fence. I soon learned some of their songs, and I stood there singing along with them. Some of them noticed me and turned a smiling face toward me. I enjoyed standing there among other kids and acting like a leader, since I knew their songs. Once in a while, my grandmother would notice me and drag me away from the fence: "Don't you understand how dangerous this is? The soldiers should not see you! You are not allowed to stand near the fence."

I would look at her and say, "But Baba, they are so nice, and they smile at me."
She would look at me, wring her hands, sigh *"Oy vey!"* and let me go.

During the day, when most of the women went out into the chilly yard to breathe some fresh air, I used to jump around on all the mattresses. I felt that things were bad because of the way in which the adults behaved, but I wanted to enjoy the fun of togetherness and the wonderful event that all these people were now sleeping in my baba's tiny house, which had stretched and changed so much. I felt sorry, however, for many of these beautiful ladies who now looked gray, battered, and frightened. They sold most of their beautiful clothes for food and looked shabby and unattended. I wanted to speak to them, to make them laugh and be happy again, but when I walked up to one of them and saw her sad and "closed" face I could not say anything.

In addition to the Romanian and German soldiers who paraded the streets, we could see many Jews carrying bundles and suitcases and walking in silence toward the train station, which was very close to the ghetto. They were walking, bent down, not looking around, and shivering in the cold October air. Looking at them frightened me, and I used to rush to Baba and say to her, "We will always stay in your tiny house, right?" She would hug me and cuddle me without saying a word.

Every day groups of people would gather their belongings, leave the Ghetto, and walk toward the train station. They all had yellow Stars of David on their clothes. I often saw my grandmother sewing such Stars of David and giving them out to people. She used to cut out two triangles of carton, cover each with yellow cloth, and then sew them together. There were always pieces of yellow material lying around, but she would not let me touch it.

Some of the older men began making yellow stars from pieces of wood, which they later painted yellow. Some of them let me paint these pieces of wood, and I was very happy working with the older men.

One morning I saw my mother wearing the yellow Star of David. She was very serious and did not look at me. Both she and Baba looked as if they had not slept all night. My mother wore her warm coat, which had a fur lining inside but looked very simple on the outside. She had a warm hat on her head and a shawl wrapped around the hat and her shoulders. She was wearing brown, old-looking boots with heavy soles and wool gloves. She had a small suitcase and a backpack of clothes, which she put on a large wagon, drawn by a horse, which was standing in the yard. Many other people were loading up the wagon. They were all very silent. They looked at each other worriedly and said nothing. Then my mother climbed on top of the suitcases on the wagon, and so did some other women. The driver of the wagon started urging the horse, and the wagon began to move very slowly. I was standing nearby, looking at my mother, and waiting for some explanation. Baba came out and hugged my shoulders with one hand, standing very close to me. She too was very silent and held her other hand on her mouth. My mother turned to me and with a big smile said, "Litika, I am going away for a short while to meet your father. I will be back very soon. Stay with Baba and be a good girl." She did not come down from the wagon and did not hug me. She simply waived to me, and I waived back. Baba and I watched the wagon drive slowly out of the ghetto and disappear in the distance.

Baba turned to me and said, "Let's go in and have a cup of tea and some bread with jam," and I followed her quietly.

All the Jews who went to the train station that day were sent to Transnistria. Transnistria was the name given by the Romanians to an area around Moghilev in the Ukraine that stretched between the Dniester River to the west, the Bug River in the east, and the Black Sea to the south. There were many small villages in this area, inhabited by Ukrainian farmers, among them a large number of Jewish families (Before the war there had been 300,000 Jews in this area, and after the war only 485 survived; the others had been murdered during the war). The Jews from Czernowitz and all of Bukovina, and later Bessarabia and Moldova, were deported to Transnistria, where they were forced to carry out heavy labor for the local communities. The deportations took place between fall of 1941 and fall of 1942. The Romanians sent the Jews away without any prior plans, and they were left to fend for themselves under conditions of hunger, lack of housing, and hardships of the cold weather. Many died of hunger, of typhoid, or of the conditions in the labor camps. My mother was sent to Transnistria on one of the early transports.

After my mother left, the ghetto began to grow smaller and smaller. Some of the people left on foot, carrying their bags and walking toward the train station, from where the deportations took place. Others were given permits to return to their homes. The Mayor of Czernowitz, Dr. Popovici, had managed to convince the Romanian governor to allow 20.000 Jews to stay in town and not be deported. These were people needed for the war efforts and included physicians, electricians, and other important professionals. Some people over the age of sixty and pregnant women were also allowed to stay.

Among the people who received permits to stay was my uncle Yossel. He was an electrician working for the municipality. Although he was considered as my baba's least bright son (Srul /"Tarzan" in Palestine was the star of the family, and he had studied medicine in Vienna, my mother was the very bright daughter, and my uncle Biyumin, who I never met, was the hard-working man). Yossel was quiet, always smiling, and resembled his father, Leizer, more than any of the others. He did not study much beyond elementary school, and I never saw him reading or writing. My baba on the other hand, although she had run away from school after second grade, was a true self-taught person and read German and Yiddish fluently. I often saw her read the newspaper, a book, or even a prayer book in Hebrew. She had worked very hard to give her children the best education possible, but Yossel had difficulties in school and was very good with his hands. So he learned the trade as a youngster and became a very skilled electrician working for the Municipality of Czernowitz. Grandmother's youngest sister Rosa Holzhaker and her family also received a permit to stay, and that gave us some comfort. They were considered a rich family living in the center of town. Nathan Holzhaker, Rosa's husband, was also an electrician and worked with Yossel, and two of their three sons, Turi and Herbert, were living at home with them.

When all the strange people left the ghetto, my grandparents stayed in their little house. Yossel managed to get a permit for his parents (my grandparents), and for the time being they were safe. He was now the only son in Czernowitz, and he was able to save his parents from the terrible transports.

Yossel came to visit his parents everyday, and he always played with me and told me stories and jokes. He also used to bring me some sweets or even a piece of cake, which was the delight of the day. Then one day he said to Baba. "Listen, why don't I take Litika home with me. She is listed as my daughter anyway. In our house it is warm, and we have a bathroom and warm running water. The winter will be much colder soon. It will be so much easier and better for her and also easier for you." I could see a tear in my grandmother's eye, but after a few minutes she agreed and packed my few things: a few dresses that were beginning to be too short for me, two pairs of shoes, some sweaters, and a warm overcoat.

I went over to her, hugged her, and sat in her lap for a while. "When will my mother be back?" I whispered to her.

She did not really answer, but she said, "Your mother will pick you up from Yossel's apartment." This sounded very promising to me, and I was ready to go.

I went with Yossel quite happily. I loved my uncle, and I knew that he would always be there for me. When we arrived at his place, a large and warm apartment in the center of town, the living room was full of people. There was my aunt Regina, of course, who was now Yossel's wife, but she was also a cousin of his and my mother (her father was one of my grandfather Leizer's many brothers). The two cousins were married, with the blessing of the family, since both had not found a partner by the age of twenty-five, and they seemed to be good friends, although not really in love. In the large living room I saw Regina's two sisters: Nora, who was even older than Regina but not married, and Mina, who was younger and the most beautiful of the three. In addition to the three sisters there were three young men sitting on the sofa in a very relaxed and cozy manner.

As we walked into the apartment, after Yossel turned two keys in the door and someone from the inside opened it, everybody greeted us. Regina looked surprised and said, "Oh, she is staying with us now. Her mother should be very happy. For once we can do something for her." What she said sounded kind, but when I looked at her face I saw a funny expression on it. I told myself that I must remember what she said and ask Baba why she had such an unpleasant expression on her face.

Yossel took me to the table and brought me something to eat. He put my things down and went to make my bed in the same room Mina and Nora slept. Nobody else seemed to pay much attention to me, but I was happy because there was a lot of talking and laughter around and it was very different from my grandmother's quiet house. I knew Regina, Nora, and Mina, my mother's cousins, from family gatherings and from the ghetto. But they never seemed to be really interested in me, so I was attached to my uncle Yossel.

The next morning I woke up and saw my aunts, Nora and Mina, asleep in their beds. Quietly I put on my dress and my shoes and went into the living room. I still had trouble tying my shoelaces, so I left them hanging. The three men were now sitting at the table, drinking tea and talking to each other in a funny language. Later I found out that they were speaking Polish. They were Jews who had escaped from the Warsaw Ghetto and were passing through Czernowitz on their way to Palestine. The Jewish community in Czernowitz was helping them and taking great risks since, if caught, they would be killed immediately and the families that hid them would be punished or deported.

I did not know who they were or why they were staying at my uncle's place. I looked for Yossel, but he had gone to work. Regina was preparing something in the kitchen and did not look at me. Finally one of the men spoke to me in German, which sounded more like Yiddish "What is your name, beautiful girl?" He said "schejne mejdale" instead of "schones madchen." I said that I was Littika and I was three and a half years old. He picked me up and put me on his knee and said, "I have a sister who is just a little bigger than you, and I taught her how to tie her shoelaces. Do you want me to teach you?" I was very pleased since I had tried many times before to tie my own shoelaces. Then he added, "My sister can also count till ten; can you count till ten?" And he started to count with me and it was a lot of fun. We counted in German of course, but his pronunciation sounded a little funny. Especially the way he said "five" made me laugh.

Finally Regina came into the living room and said, "Ah, you are up. Are you hungry? What does your mother usually give you to eat in the morning? You know that these are hard times and we only have some black bread with jam, so this is what I am going to give you." I did not say anything. I was not sure what she expected me to say so I remained silent, but the other men started asking me questions and making jokes, and I was very happy to be with them.

Suddenly somebody rang the doorbell, and I was sure this was my mother. So I ran to the door and tried to open it, but of course I could not. Before I knew it, Regina was on top of me hitting me over the head and the face and dragging me back to the living room. "You should never, never go to the door. Do you understand?" By then I was sobbing desperately, and I ran to my bed. My two aunts had jumped out of bed as soon as they heard the doorbell, and they were standing in their nightgowns very pale and frightened. The three men had disappeared, and where there had been a door to another large room there was now a wooden wall and a cupboard. Finally Regina opened the door a bit to find out who it was; one of the neighbors said something and left.

Regina dragged me back into the living room and said to me in a loud voice, "You are not allowed to go near the door. Do you understand? Nobody is allowed into the house, and you are not allowed to talk to anybody, about anything. Do you understand that? I hit you a bit now because I was so mad at you, but if you don't listen to what I say I will hit you much harder." I could not stop sobbing. I had never been hit before, and no one ever spoke to me like Regina. The three men came back from their hiding and were sitting in the living room, but I went back to my bed and played alone for a while. Then when my eyes dried up and I caught my breath again, I went into the living room and told everybody "My mother is coming to pick me up, and I am waiting for her."

They all looked at me and smiled, and I heard Regina whisper to one of the men, "Her mother is in Transnistria."

In the evening my uncle Yossel finally came home. I felt like my "rescuer" had finally arrived. He brought me a big piece of pecan cake, which was delicious, but I really did not feel that hungry. I ate it all because I very much wanted to please him and make him feel good. Before he put me in bed for the night I asked him, "When do you think my mother will come to pick me up?"

He looked at me and said, "Why, aren't you happy here?" and I just said, "I miss my mother" and went to sleep.

A few days went by, and I continued spending time mostly with the Polish refugees. Then one day my grandmother came to visit me. I was so happy! I hugged her and clung to her all the time. Finally she said, "You should be a good girl and listen to your aunts. This home is very good for you, and you have everything here," but all I wanted to know was when my mother would pick me up and take me home.

One day my aunt Nora decided that I was very dirty and I needed a good washing. "Schmutzig" is the word she used, and I was very insulted because I knew this was a bad word. She took my clothes off and put me in a big pail of water and started scrubbing me. The water was cold and she was hurting me, so I started to cry. She got really mad at me and said I should stop immediately before she really hit me, and then I would have a good reason to cry. She dried my body with a coarse towel and said, "Now we need to take care of this tangled up dirty hair of yours." She brought a small bucket of water, stood behind me holding my body in place with her two powerful legs, and pushed my head into the bucket, bending me in half and rubbing my scalp forcefully. I was shocked and my body was petrified from the cold and her hold, and I stopped breathing. Finally the ordeal was over. She helped me put on some clean clothes, brushed my hair forcefully with a big brush, and brought me into the living room very proudly. "Now, here is a clean girl. Somebody had to take care of her." And she sat me down on the couch near one of the Polish men.

I could see that he felt sorry for me, and he hugged me and placed me on his knee and said, "You know what, my beautiful girl, I have a present for you." He took out a little box with a pair of small earrings with three little blue stones. "This will bring you good luck." Gently he pushed the earrings into my pierced ears (it was customary to pierce a girl's ears soon after she was born), and soon I was happy again. I never took off these lovely earrings until I lost one of them at the age of six.

One day when I woke up in the morning, the three men were gone and two other men were sitting there. They were sad and looked frightened and did not even notice me. After the daily curfew (Jews were allowed to walk on the streets of Czernowitz only for a few hours during the day), my grandmother came to visit. This time I cried bitterly and asked her to take me back with her: "I don't want to live here with my aunts. I want to be with you and Grandpa." She explained to me that their house was cold in the winter and I would be very bored with two old people who have nothing and where the food is not so good.

"Who will bring you good cakes in the evening? And who will play with you all day?"

I continued crying and sobbing, and I said, "I don't care I want to be with you". My Baba could not see me like this and finally she took me home with her. All the way home she tried to explain to me how fortunate I was to have Uncle Yossel and Aunt Regina, who are like parents to me. I just listened and said nothing.

# Chapter Four

# Living with Baba

Life in my grandparents' small house, in the now deserted ghetto, was quiet and uneventful. It was a cold and bitter winter, and we rarely left the house. Most of the day I sat curled up near the stove and covered up with blankets. The snow outside came up to the door, and the windows were frozen in the morning looking like brilliant crystals with the most intricate shapes and figures carved in the ice. I could look at these shapes for hours and imagine people, animals, and trees. Clothes that were hung out after washing turned to icicles over night and had to be thawed out near the stove. I heard people say that this was one of the colder winters they remembered.

Once in a while my grandmother would leave the house during the hours when there was no curfew in order to do some shopping or to visit her sister Rosa or her son Yossel. Nobody came to visit us, and I always wanted to go with her and not stay alone with my grandfather, but it was too cold, my good shoes were getting to be too small on me, and my winter coat was too short, and so I just had to stay home.

Once or twice a week Maria, a former maid who had worked for my grandmother in better times, used to come and visit us. She always brought some work for my grandmother: mending old clothes, sewing something new from old material, or shortening and lengthening dresses that she had collected from various people. In return for my grandmother's beautiful work she used to bring us black bread and fresh butter and sometimes some jam. We usually ate *mamaliga* (the Romanian word for corn polenta) three times a day: cold slices of *mamaliga* in the morning with jam, hot *mamaliga* with a little butter for lunch, and some more *mamaliga* in the evening. Sometimes my grandmother cooked potatoes, and that was delicious.

When Maria brought the black bread it was a real celebration. My Baba cut a nice thick slice for me, covered it with plenty of butter, and then cut it in very small squares. On each little square she placed a small piece of garlic. This was particularly suitable for the *jause* (afternoon tea) of the day. There was no sugar, no cakes, and no coffee or tea for the daily *jause,* but Baba always liked to have *jause* with whatever we had in the house. I used to take a long time eating each square of buttered bread and garlic, savoring the taste and trying to keep the memory of it for days when we had no bread, at all. The *jause* was also the time Baba told me one of my favorite stories either from the German tradition, like Little Red Riding Hood, Snow White, and Cinderella (Aschenbredl), which was my favorite, or stories from the Bible such as Joseph and the Colored Coat, the story about Yaakov, Rachel, and Leah, David and Goliath, or Samson the heroic. She was a wonderful storyteller and always made everything sound interesting and mysterious.

Baba had been a beautiful young woman before she married, the oldest of three very strong, bright, and independent sisters in the Rosenbaum family who lived in the outskirts of Czernowitz. They spoke German at home, and all their children, except my Baba Sabina, had been well educated and married well. Tante Sofie was the middle sister, and she was the brightest of the three. She finished high school and spoke German, Romanian, and

French. She had *Matura* (the end of high school certificate). Everybody respected and loved her. She had married a rich man, and they were the pride of the family. My mother's dream had always been to be like Tante Sofie. Unfortunately, however, Tante Sofie had cancer and died just before I was born.

Tante Rosa was the youngest and the shrewdest of the three and was known for her selfishness and lack of consideration for others. She had married a reticent and withdrawn electrician who worked for the municipality, like my Uncle Yossel. Tante Rosa ran an electrical shop and made good money. They were in general well off and owned a large building with three floors in the center of town. Baba Sabina, on the other hand, had very limited formal education since in the second grade of elementary school she decided one day to go to the river Prut with some friends instead of going to school. The following day she was scolded and sent home, after which she was too embarrassed to go back to school. Her mother thought that education was important even for girls, but since Sabina already knew how to read and write German and was also good in basic arithmetic, she could stay home and help raise the younger children and tend the farm. Her help was especially important with the little baby brother, Herman. Sabina, however, never stopped studying on her own. She perfected her German, read books, and studied Romanian and Ukrainian.. She also asked her father to teach her the Hebrew letters so she could read and write in Yiddish, and she read many of the authors of the time who wrote in Yiddish.

Sabina was the quiet and subservient sister who always worked on her parents' farm and in the house while her sisters spent most of their time in town. So it was natural for her two younger sisters to be married before she was. She was soon considered an "old maid." One day a very handsome young soldier stopped in their village and asked for some help with his horse. He was a horseman in the Austrian army, and his name was Liezer Furman. His education was extremely limited, in fact he hardly knew how to read, but he spoke nicely to Sabina's parents, and he seemed like a nice Jewish boy. He watched Sabina do the house chores and fell in love with her. They soon got married, and Sabina's parents were happy to finally send their oldest daughter to build a life of her own.

The match was a pretty miserable one. Still, as long as Liezer was getting the salary from the Austrian army they managed to raise their four children: Byumin, Srul, Yossel, and Frieda. Thus they survived the Great War (the first World War), but then the Austrian army stopped paying Liezer the good salary that he had earned, and he became a horse trader. He was not a very industrious person, did not really make a living, and could not support his family. The burden of making ends meet fell upon Sabina, who was clever and capable and always found ways to make some money. She bought and sold things, she traded, she sewed, she mended, and she undertook many different jobs enabling her to raise her four children. She managed to give all of them a pretty good education and all the basics of the time. But everyone knew that the Furmans were really quite poor. Still Byumin, who liked agriculture, bought himself a farm in one of the villages near Czernowitz and started his family there. Srul was an excellent student at school, and Sabina saved every penny for years and sent him to study medicine in Vienna, yet he abandoned his studies and left for Palestine to build a new kibbutz there. He was inspired by Zionist leaders who spoke to the Jewish students in Vienna, and he felt that his calling was to become a farmer in Palestine for the Zionist cause rather than become a physician and stay in Europe. Yossel became a skilled electrician, and Frieda completed her studies at a Hebrew Teachers' College for girls "Safra Ivriya." My grandmother Sabina could be proud of her family.

Now, following the Nazi takeover, like in many other families in Czernowitz her children were scattered in very different places: Byumin and Frieda were in Transnistria, Srul was in Palestine, and only Yossel stayed in town, and she could see him once in a while.

My grandparents were the only Jewish family who was still living in the ghetto area, one of the poorest neighborhoods in town. Most of the other Jewish families who had lived there had been deported to Transnistria.

As for myself, I felt that I was fortunate to be with my grandparents, especially my Baba whom I loved dearly. Since I had no real toys to play with, my grandmother used to make me dolls and stuffed animals made of rags and pieces of old clothing. She taught me how to sing children's songs in German and how to recite various short rhymes. My grandfather, on the other hand, slept most of the day or took care of some chores around the house. He rarely spoke to me, and when he looked at me I always felt as if he wanted to say, "Who is this little girl? What is she doing here? Why isn't she with her parents?" I didn't really care since I was happy to live with Baba, but I missed my parents, especially my mother.

"When will my mother come back?" I used to ask my grandmother. "Why did she leave like this without saying goodbye?" My grandmother would explain to me that my mother had no choice and that she did not say goodbye because she did not want to make me sad.

"I know she is thinking about you every minute, and I know she will come back to you one day. We must be strong and keep healthy and wait for that day." I listened to her, and I felt that she was right. I often made a decision for myself that I was to be wise and strong like my Baba.

During the cold nights of that winter I slept in the middle of the big bed with my grandmother on one side and my grandfather on the other. This kept me warm and happy. We would all go to bed soon after it got dark and wake up at daylight. In spite of the poverty all around me and in spite of being there without my parents, I was far from being miserable. But then, one night I woke up feeling very cold. I was all alone in the large bed. I could hear terrible screams and strange loud voices. I sat up to see what was happening and felt my body become stiff with fear. My grandmother was standing in her thin nightgown in front of one the windows. The glass was shattered, and she was taking my mother's things out of her cupboard and placing them into someone's arms reaching into the room through the window. I could see the glitter of the silver candlesticks and the beautifully embroidered tablecloths. Whenever she hesitated, a long pipe would be pushed through the window from someone on the outside, and Baba would be hit with it. She cried out painfully with every blow and brought out more things. My eyes searched for my grandfather, whose voice I could hear constantly screaming *"Gewald, gewald!"* He was standing at the door, propping up various pieces of furniture in an attempt to resist the blows coming from the outside. It was a terrible sight and I could do nothing!

I drew the big down blanket over my head and lay still in bed. I knew I had to be very quiet so no one would notice me. The screaming went on for a long time, and then suddenly there was a roaring voice coming from the top of the hill "Stop that immediately or I will call the police." The attackers grabbed everything my grandmother had given them through the window and ran away. Everything became very quiet, but I could hear my grandmother's sobs and my grandfather crying like a little child. I slowly lowered the blanket and crawled out so I could look around. Baba was sitting on the floor in a pool of broken glass and sobbing so deeply that her whole body shook. My grandfather was sitting on a chair with a big hayfork in his hand and was crying with low and subdued sighs. A cold wind was coming through the broken window, and I was worried and frightened because they did not seem to notice me at all.

The three of us sat like this for a long time, and I was too frightened to say anything. Suddenly my grandmother stood up and looked at me as if she noticed me for the first time. She came over and hugged me and said: *"Mein Schatz, Mein Oytzer* ("my treasure" in German and in Yiddish). We must save you. You must live and be safe." When my grandmother was excited she used both languages at the same time. Her words frightened me even more, because I did not really understand what she meant.

In a short while the three of us were dressed, and two little bundles of clothes were lying on the bed. The dull winter morning was just breaking when someone knocked at the door. The three of us jumped and our hearts were beating wildly. It turned out to be Maria who was unusually early this morning. "What happened here?" she said in surprise. My grandmother told her that some Romanian hooligans attacked us and took everything we had. She showed her the empty cupboards, and then she showed her the black and blue marks across her body from the beating she had taken. Maria stood there wringing her hands.

"Ivan, our neighbor from the top of the hill saved us. He shouted at the hooligans and chased them away." Finally Baba said that she was giving Maria the keys for the little house since we were leaving to stay with some family in town.

As Maria left, Baba said to grandfather: "I have a strong feeling that Maria sent the hooligans to frighten us and rob us. They probably were not going to kill us, but thank God for Ivan's kind heart and loud voice. None of the other neighbors, who live much closer to us, said or did anything. Ivan's voice certainly chased them away."

It was still quite dark and very chilly outside, but Baba said that she and I had to leave right away, without waiting for the end of the curfew when Jews were allowed to be outside. Grandfather would come and join us a little later. "Where are we going?" I asked, worried that we might be going to Yossel and Regina again.

"We are going to Tante Rosa. I hope that she will find a little room for us in her big house. We have no other choice." I did not know Tante Rosa very well, but I knew she was my Baba's younger sister and that sounded good.

We left the house and the yard very quietly. Baba took me through some small streets that looked completely deserted at this early time of day. Whenever we heard the sound of walking or the trot of a horse, we would quickly hide in one of the alleys or yards. German and Romanian soldiers were patrolling the streets, making sure no Jew broke the curfew. Thus, slowly and painfully, with my grandmother limping because she had stepped on a piece of glass and her ankle began to swell and me limping because my shoes were too small and my toes hurt, we finally arrived at Tante Rosa's house. This was a large three story building on one of the more beautiful streets of Czernowitz.

Although we had walked for two hours, it was still early in the morning, and the curfew was still on. We climbed the stairs to the first floor, where Tante Rosa and her family lived and knocked on the door. It took a few minutes until someone finally opened the door. Tante Rosa stood in the doorway in a nightgown and housecoat. She looked extremely surprised to see us and hesitated for a moment but let us into the living room. It was a large room with a beautiful candelabrum in the center and a large table with chairs underneath it. Soon the whole family gathered in the living room, Oncle Natan, Tury, who was nineteen, and Herbert, who was seventeen. Baba told her story and showed them all her blue and black marks across her body. I wondered why she was not ashamed to lift her blouse and skirt and show them the marks, but she seemed too excited to answer any of my questions. They all listened in shock, but nobody rushed to her to hug her or comfort her. Tante Rosa finally said, "Well as you know we are living here now, Nathan and I and our two sons, Tury and Herbert. We don't have much room, but Tury could move into Herbert's room, and you could have Tury's room for the time being." Baba took off her shoe, and her left foot did not look good—it was swollen and red.

Tury and Herbert hurried into the room and fixed the bed for Baba. She finally laid down and closed her eyes. I stood there and waited for someone to notice me. Tury was the first to come to me. He helped me take off my coat and wet shoes, and then he sat me down on a chair in the kitchen and made me *"ein Spiegel eye"* (a sunny side up egg) with some bread and butter. I had not had eggs for a long time, and I enjoyed every bite of my bread dipped in the yellow yoke. Then I went to Baba and sat near her on her bed. "Now I will tell you stories, and you can rest," I said to her. By noon my grandfather arrived, and the three of us settled into Tury's room, which was pleasant and warm and had a window facing the street. I felt that I could be happy and comfortable here. I did not think Tante Rosa cared much for me, but I felt that Tury and Herbert liked me. I knew that they would soon be my best friends.

My grandparents never went back to their little house, and we never heard from Maria again.

# Chapter Five

# Life at Tante Rosa's

The night after arriving at Tante Rosa's house was sleepless. The three of us were lying in a bed, which was much smaller than the bed we had in the small house. Baba was sighing all night—she was suffering terrible pain and could not sleep. My grandfather was sitting on a chair for most of the night, dozing off now and then and jumping up from his sleep with a groan. We kept the electrical light on all night, since we were so happy to have electrical light again after the gas light in the little house. I could not sleep because I was worried about my Baba, and I thought that I should pray. I heard people praying to God, but I did not know how. It was the end of February 1942 and I was almost four years old, but I did not know how you pray to God.

The next morning Tante Rosa came in to see how her sister was doing. She touched her forehead and a scream came out of her mouth: "My God, you are burning up. You have a very high temperature, and we must call Dr. Pistiner." Toward noon the nice Jewish doctor arrived. He was a smiling man with a short white beard. He brought some pills for Baba to take and he looked at her leg for a long time. Finally he asked Tante Rosa to bring a big pail with warm water and have Baba sit with her leg in warm water. He told them to repeat this treatment for a few days, and then he would come again to see how things were. He said to Baba, looking around the room, "In these hard times you should feel content that you have this lovely room to rest in and a sister to take care of you. Try to sleep and eat and take care of your leg until that nasty piece of glass comes out." Then he looked at me and said, smiling, "Little girl, do you know how to sing and dance? Cheer up your grandmother so she will get better soon."

When he left I felt very happy. I embraced Baba, and I said to her, "My prayers were answered, and you are going to get better".

Tante Rosa looked at me and said with a sad expression on her face, "Just four years old and is already talking like a grown up. This is a shame!" Tante Rosa's words echoed in my head—"She talks like an *alte mojd*." I knew she did not like me.

All day long I tried to sing and dance for my Baba and tell her the stories I remembered. Finally my grandfather looked at me in anger and said, "Shut up a little; you are making so much noise I can't sleep". So I went to the window and sat there for a long time looking at the people walking fast in the cold. All the buildings on the other side of the street were covered with snow, and they looked like castles in a fairy tale. I was just a little sad: *If my mother were here*, I thought, *she would take care of Baba and of me, and we could be very happy*.

I waited all day for Tury and Herbert to come home. When they finally arrived, I could see Herbert was nervous. He told everybody that he hoped his girlfriend Sylvia would come by at night, although it was very dangerous to walk the streets at night. Again it was Tury who was nice to me. He brought cheese, pastrami, and fresh bread, and the whole family sat down to eat. My grandparents were not part of this celebration. They had had a little soup to eat during the day and were basically staying in their room. I, on the other hand, felt like part of the family because Tury fed me, talked to me, told me some funny rhymes in

German, and altogether made me very happy. Suddenly there was a loud and impatient knock on the door, and Sylvia entered the house sobbing and crying. She had walked from her house to Tante Rosa's when suddenly she noticed two Romanian soldiers running after her. They were drunk and were shouting obscenities at her, but she ran as fast as she could and managed to escape.

Herbert took her by the hand and sat with her in the living room on the sofa for a long time. Tury noticed that I did not want to go to sleep at all, so he took me into their room and he pushed some chairs together and made me a little bed where I could sleep. He said, "Don't worry about Baba. She took some pills, and she will sleep well now, and you can stay here for tonight or for any night that you choose" I had eaten well, I had enjoyed the lively talk at the dinner table with the electrical light on everywhere, and I was content. That night I slept very well.

The following days and nights went by in a similar way. Baba was still in bed and could not walk. My grandfather dozed off in his chair while the others were going out of the house to their jobs, chores, and other occupations. Uncle Nathan, Tante Rosa's husband, went to work at the electrical plant every morning. Tury and Herbert went to work in the forced labor camp near Czernowitz. They always left very early in the morning and came back very late in the evening. The doctor came again and tried to squeeze Baba's ankle in an attempt to push the piece of glass out but to no avail. More days went by with Baba getting very impatient and saying again and again: "I cannot stay in bed and be nursed all the time. I must get up and do something, but I cannot stand on my foot."

My birthday came and went, but no one remembered it except for Tury, who brought me a doll. This doll became my best friend, and I told her everything. I sat for hours near the window, talking to her and looking at the people in the street. I always waited impatiently for the evening when Tury and Hebert would come back and bring good food to eat and exciting stories to tell.

Sometimes my uncle Yossel would come for a brief visit and bring some food for the family. He always had a piece of cake for me.

One evening as we were sitting and waiting for Tury and Herbert to come home, Baba squeezed her ankle as usual after the foot bath and suddenly she cried out with joy, "The glass is out,; the glass is out!" and she was holding a piece of glass the size of an olive pit in her hand. Everybody came rushing to her bed, and we were all very happy.

"A few more days," said Tante Rosa, "and you will be able to stand on your own two feet, and then we should make some plans. But first we will celebrate the Seder together."

The next day Baba was happier than I had seen her for a long time. She tried to comb out my tangled-up hair with a lot of patience. She was talking to me again the way she used to in the little house. This seemed like a good time to ask her some questions that bothered me about our family: Why were some of the women so cruel and so strict with me—Tante Regina, Tante Nora, Tante Rosa. She looked at me for a long time and then sighed and said, "Littika, you are still a little girl, only four years old, but I think I should explain a few things to you. You see, Frieda, your mother has always been beautiful and clever. Everything she did was always excellent: she was a very good student, she received prizes in German and History, her Romanian is good, she studied French and Hebrew. Tante Sofie loved her best from all her nieces, and she always brought her nice clothes from her frequent trips to Vienna. Frieda was in Hashomer Hatzair, the only girl in our family, and Srul introduced her to the best boys and girls in town. Although your mother was very poor she always mixed with the rich and the powerful. Then of course she met Willy, who was an excellent match, and she got married and moved up in society. Now look at Nora; she passed the age of thrity and never had a boyfriend, Regina ended up marrying Yossel, a cousin, who was not exactly the success in the family. And Mina is dying to find a husband, and that is why she is always talking to the Poles in their apartment, putting on her best clothes and makeup. These are three cousins of your mother's who have envied her bitterly since childhood. They see you, and they remember that you are Frieda's daughter and they don't have to like you."

I thought of Cinderella and her cruel sisters, and I thought I understood what my grandmother was saying.

Baba tried to explain why we could not stay forever with Tante Rosa. "She is my sister, but she always treated me as the poor part of our family. In her eyes I was not successful in marriage or in life in general. In her eyes this is my own fault. She knew better, and she did better for herself. Now we are here, and we are eating her food, sleeping in her bed, and she even has to nurse me since I am helpless with this foot. She does not like this at all, and she can't wait for us to find some other solution".

I did not understand the word "solution," but I knew Baba would think of something. I also thought that my wonderful Baba, who was clever and beautiful and warm and wise, should be loved by everyone. How could her sister be so mean to her?

The following week was exciting. Somehow Rosa was able to buy *mazahs* for the Seder and even bought some fish. So on the Seder night the whole family gathered around the large table in the living room. Uncle Nathan and my grandfather were both sitting at the head of the table on large pillows that were placed in their seats. There was a white and beautiful tablecloth on the table, and everything looked very special. I sat between Tury and Herbert and looked at the Haggada book with them. Tury showed me all the pictures and explained the story. He said that the Haggada was a beautiful book and I should take this copy and look through it whenever I am sad. The Haggada book became my friend for many years to come.

Baba slowly began to walk again and soon gained back her strength and good mood. I told myself that I must always be careful with broken glass since it can be so terrible. To this day I get hysterical if anything breaks in the house.

Baba began to leave the house during the hours when the curfew was off to look for ways to make some money. She always wore her yellow Star of David on her coat. *I* had to stay home since I had no shoes or warm clothes. The spring was slow in coming, and although some of the snow had melted it was still quite cold outside.

One day I was sitting at the window and hugging my doll, as usual. I was looking at the tall trees outside now full of new, green foliage. On the other side of the street I could see a beautiful lilac bush all in purple attire. How I wanted to touch and smell that purple! The lilacs were blooming, but I could not go out because I had no warm clothes or shoes to wear. Butterflies were prancing in the sun, and everything looked happy and pleasant. My grandmother was in the kitchen baking rolls (her latest occupation), and my grandfather was asleep as always. I was alone facing that beautiful world outside, which I could not touch. I felt locked up in a cage, a cage made of cold glass that had this unreal image on the outside. Were the butterflies real? Was it warm or cold outside? Will I ever be able to touch those green leaves outside and smell the blooming lilac bush?

In the evening I was waiting for Herbert and Tury as usual. But this time they came home in a very bad mood and hardly spoke to me. I felt that I had to be quiet and not be seen or heard. Tante Rosa was crying and walking around the living room nervously. Baba sat on a chair in the corner and held her hand tightly to her mouth. Something was very bad. I just sat and watched the worried grownups. Finally Tante Rosa said, "Tury and Herbert, you must go to sleep because you have to get up and go to work tomorrow as usual. During the day I will pack your things, and we will all be ready".

During the next day no one wanted to speak to me, and everybody said, "Be quiet. You are a little girl, and you should not ask so many questions!" Baba came back from her roll-selling trip and brought me a pair of shoes. She told me that in one of the houses where she sold the rolls, there was a girl a little bit bigger than me, and she asked the lady for some old shoes that were too small for her little girl. I tried them on, and they felt good. I was so happy and danced around the house in my new shoes, but soon everybody sent me away to a corner and told me to be quiet. Tante Rosa was busy all day packing and sewing things and baking cookies. When Tury and Herbert came home they changed clothes quickly, ate something in the kitchen, and seemed to be ready for some secret adventure. Baba explained to me that they were leaving to go to Palestine, but nobody should know about it.

"It is a very big secret!" she said to me. Late at night, when Tury and Herbert were ready to go, Tante Rosa and Baba were also ready to go with them.

"I want to go too, to see off Tury and Herbert!" I cried, and Baba said quickly that since I had a pair of shoes now, I could come along. We left quietly, walking very silently through the dark streets until we reached the train station. There the train was ready to leave for the seaport, where Tury and Herbert would board a ship going to Palestine. We said goodbye to them very quietly. Big tears were covering Tante Rosa's face, but she did not say a word. Herbert and Tury were on the train, but the train did not move for a long time, although the windows and doors of the train were shut and the noise of the engine made us think that at any moment the train would leave the station. The minutes were passing by slowly, and the train did not move. Tante Rosa, started sobbing, and suddenly there was a siren. We all huddled up in a corner. Everything was quiet, and there were some distant sounds of artillery. Tante Rosa said, "Oh, my God. They are going to bombard the train, and my two boys will be killed." But suddenly the train began to move slowly, the whistle blew loud and clear, and within a few minutes the train was gone. We all sighed with relief and made our way home in the darkness of the night. Later I understood that Tury and Herbert were going illegally to

Palestine. They had managed to get papers that would allow them to travel within Romania and then continue on a boat to Palestine to join my uncle Srul on his kibbutz. I knew that I would never forget that night.

# Chapter Six

# The Yellow Star of David

Tante Rosa's house was quiet and empty now. Everybody was sad, and I missed Tury and Herbert. The Nazis and the Romanian army were rounding up Jews again to send more transports to Transnistria. Every time we heard about these transports, Tante Rosa said, "Thank God my boys left before they were caught." One day some policemen came to the house looking for Tury and Herbert. They shouted and hit Tante Rosa when she said that she did not know where they were. Then she opened a drawer and took out some money and put it on the table. The policemen took the money and left the house. A few weeks later we got a postcard from Palestine. Srul informed us that "the delivery was made," and so we knew that Tury and Herbert arrived safely.

    We were still living in the same bedroom, the three of us, but Baba was more and more tense and said that we must find some other solution. She was buying flour and yeast at the market and baking rolls everyday, which she sold by going from home to home, from door to door. One summer day, I told her that I was going to go with her, that I did not want to stay home anymore. After a lot of crying and pleading she said, "Okay, you can come with me, but I warn you, you will get tired, and I don't have time to stop. I must finish selling all the rolls before the curfew." I was very happy, and I put on one of my baby spring dresses, which Baba had lengthened by adding some material to it. I put on my new shoes, and we set out to sell the rolls. As we stepped into the street Baba suddenly realized that I did not have a yellow Star of David on me. She said, "Don't walk too close to me so that the policemen won't notice that you belong to me." I looked at her, and I felt very insulted. How could my Baba tell me to act as if I did not belong to her? I did not say anything, but I looked at her accusingly. Finally we reached the street where rich people lived and where she knocked on every door and sold her rolls. I was standing behind her, glancing at the rich ladies who did not treat Baba very nicely. Soon I got very tired, and I pleaded with her to let me sit on the sidewalk just for a minute. "I told you that I must finish selling all the rolls and I cannot stop now—you must try to walk even if you are tired." Finally she finished the batch of rolls, and we had just a little time to go to the market and buy some more flour and some bread. We were both pleased, and we forgot all about the yellow Star of David. She took my hand, and we walked through the narrow alleys of the market.

It was a very warm day, and the sun blinded me. Suddenly I heard a loud voice speaking to my grandmother, and when I looked up I could see a large policeman with a big moustache sneering at her: "So, where is the little girl's yellow star?" My grandmother started trembling, and she began to explain that it fell on the way. He began screaming at her. "I can deport you both to Transnistria for this!". My grandmother quickly took out all the money she had made that day selling rolls, and gave it to the policeman. He took the money quickly and said, "Go home woman and make some more yellow stars. Next time you won't get off that easily."

We both walked very quickly from the market through the back streets to Tante Rosa's house. Baba said nothing, but I felt terrible. I knew that I had spoiled her day—first I made it hard for her to sell the rolls quickly, and then she had to pay all this money to the policeman. If I had stayed home none of this would have happened. I never joined her again on the roll-selling trips.

When we got home, Baba took a piece of carton and cut a number of triangles. She found some yellow cloth and showed me how to sew it on and then make it into a Star of David. "From now on we will always have an additional Star of David in our pocket so that what happened today will never happen again," she said.

A few weeks later Tante Rosa had an idea. There was a small apartment on the roof of her building. It needed cleaning and a few pieces of furniture, but we could move in there and stay for the rest of the war. She also had a solution for a meager income for our family—we could rent out one of the rooms to an old man who would pay us for room and board, and Baba could cook and clean for him. A small part of the rent would go back to Tante Rosa, and the rest would allow us to survive these hard times. So we moved again, and a new era began. Baba was pleased with the arrangement, and whispered to me, Srul is helping Tante Rosa's sons in Palestine, and she is helping us here.

The roof apartment was quite comfortable. It had two small bedrooms and one larger living room/corridor area with a cooking corner and a small bathroom. As soon as we moved in, we were joined by an old and grumpy man who moved into the bedroom with the window to the main street. His name was Mr Katz. He was a religious person. He stayed in his room almost all the time, reading and praying all day long. Three times a day my grandmother would bring him food. Once in a while he would come out of his room in order to let my grandmother clean it.

Mr. Katz always seemed annoyed and angry. He never spoke to me except for scolding me and telling me that I made much too much noise and he could not concentrate on his work. He was not very kind or friendly to my grandmother, but she did not seem to mind. One day as I was sitting near the table where she prepared his food and mended his shirts, I asked her: "Why do we have to live with this Mr Katz who is always so grumpy?"

She looked at me sadly and said, "He is really a good man, but he lost his family, and he is all alone. We take care of him, and he pays us very good rent so that we can buy food and stay in this apartment. That is why we must be very nice to him. Whenever he comes out of the room you should go into our bedroom and be very quiet. And when you are playing here in the living room remember that he can hear you through the door."

"But I want to sing and dance like always!" I protested.

"Well, sing in whispers, and dance on your tippy-toes so that he cannot hear you," she answered.

We lived like this for over a year and a half. It was basically comfortable, and we always had some food to eat. My grandmother would cook the best food for Mr. Katz and mostly *mamaliga* for us. At the beginning I loved *mamaliga*, especially when it was freshly cooked and we had some butter to spread on it. But after a while I began hating it. We ate it for breakfast, lunch, and dinner. Most of the time it was cold slices with some jam on it. I could not look at it anymore.

During this year and a half I became a pale and scrawny little girl of almost six. I seldom left the house, and I never met any children my age. I was always sitting with my grandmother, who taught me lots of rhymes and songs in German. I knew how to count, and I knew to recite the letters in German and in Yiddish. My only doll was turning into a terrible looking rag, and I often painted my knee as a face and wrapped a scarf around it to make it look like a doll.

Since I was bigger now, my grandmother talked to me more about my parents. She explained that we didn't know if my father was still alive because we hadn't heard from him since the war started. My mother was in a camp called "Transnistria," and we did not hear from her either. Every now and then some neighbor or relative would come to visit and would tell my grandmother that "So and so was gone since they took him over the Bug" (*uber den Buk*). I tried to imagine what that sentence meant. I thought that the Bug was a bridge, and some people were taken on that bridge to the other side of the river and then they were lost. Years later I found out that the Bug was a river north of Transnistria where hundreds of Jews were thrown off a cliff and killed.

One day I asked my grandmother, "Baba, is my mother going to be taken over the Bug?" She looked shocked and quickly said that she was sure that my mother Frieda was okay and we would hear from her soon. Then one day a postcard arrived, and my Baba was so happy that she cried and laughed at the same time. "Your mother is alive. She is alright," she kept saying and holding the postcard to the light, trying to read it, but that was impossible. I did not yet know how to read, but I could see that there was a short line at the top and a short line at the bottom but all the longer lines in between were crossed out with black ink. "Your mother wrote "Dear family" and signed "Yours, Frieda," and the rest we cannot read because the censor erased it, but it does not matter. We know that she is alive, and soon the war will end and she will come back to you." I was happy, but I was also very sad. I could not wait so long for my mother; I wanted her home right away.

One day the sirens blew louder than ever. We could hear planes in the sky and explosions in the distance. It was late in December of 1943. Tante Rosa came up to our apartment, which she never did, and said that we must all go to the shelter in the house across the street because there was no shelter in our house. Everybody seemed happy: "The Germans are retreating. They are losing the war, and they are bombarding the city while retreating." We all went down to the shelters with smiles rather than fear because this was the sign of the end of the war.

Only Mr. Katz did not want to go to the shelter. "I will stay in my room, no matter what happens," he said.

We sat all night in the shelter and heard the terrible sounds. Nobody slept. The women brought some food. They were talking and telling stories, and it looked as if everybody was happy to hear the explosions. Tante Rosa said, "I hope they won't hit our building with Mr. Katz in it." To me this sounded funny; I imagined the building coming down on top of us and grumpy Mr. Katz flying in the air.

After a few days of Baba going up to the apartment to bring some food and feed Mr. Katz and the rest of us staying in the shelter, people started saying that you could see the Germans going through the city: "They look shabby and sick. Some of the officers don't have cars anymore and are sitting on top of wagons drawn by horses. They look like a defeated army with nothing left."

Finally everybody got used to the sirens and the bombing, and we all decided to go back to the apartment. The New Year had gone by without us feeling it. It was now January of 1944. Then one day Baba said, "The war is about to end, and we must make sure that we get back your parents' apartment on Franzensgasse."

# Chapter Seven

# We Are Back at Our Apartment

One evening in January 1944, Baba and I went to the apartment on Franzensgasse. It was dark and cold outside, and we walked very quickly. Baba was very quiet and did not speak to me the entire time. I didn't know where we were going, but I felt that we were on a very important mission since she dressed me carefully, combed my hair, and put a ribbon in my braid. I was almost six years old, and it was the first time I remember being "dressed up."

I did no recognize the street at first, but when we started walking up the stairs my heart began to pound heavily. This was my parents' apartment. We reached the door on the second floor and stood silently listening. It seemed very quiet. Then my grandmother knocked on the door several times. The door opened, and a young German soldier stood looking at us. Baba said, "We would like to see the officer." She spoke in perfect German, of course. The soldier led us in. As we were walking down the corridor I could see a strange and unfamiliar hat rack. Then suddenly my nostrils were filled with the smell of scrambled eggs fried in butter. What a wonderful smell! I felt completely intoxicated.

The door to the living room was open, but it was dark inside, and as I peeked in I saw it was completely empty. Then I looked into the lit up kitchen and saw the soldier standing at our big stove and fixing the eggs in a frying pan. There was a plate and some cutlery on the kitchen table. Suddenly as we were standing there, the German officer came out of my parents' bedroom. He was tall and very handsome but had a stern look on his face. He looked at us and did not smile. My grandmother quickly said in German, "This little girl was born in this apartment. It belongs to her parents, and we want to move back in here when you leave."

The officer looked at us for a long time, and for a moment I thought that he did not understand my grandmother. Then he said in a very loud voice: "Old woman, take the child and get out of here. I can *still* send you to Transnistria." My Baba smiled politely, and we left right away. I was still trying to breathe in the smell of the scrambled eggs. Even today, sixty years later, I can still smell it. It always makes me feel good and optimistic.

We walked quietly back to Tante Rosa's building. Baba said, "This was very good what we just did. He cannot send us to Transnistria; the war is almost over. We have to come back here in a few days and make sure that no one else moves into the apartment before we do. It belongs to your parents, and they should get it back when they return. Thank God we know that your mother is alive."

I listened to her, but all I could think about was that menacing hat rack and the wonderful smell of scrambled eggs. To this day whenever I make scrambled eggs the same intoxicating feeling comes back to me, just for a second. But when I see a hat rack I can hear the German officer's voice telling us to get out. I never wanted a hat rack in my house, even when most of our friends owned such racks.

Eventually the Germans and their wagons disappeared and instead, the Russians came in on *their* shabby wagons. The bombing was still going on, and somebody said, "The Germans were bombing our city on their way out, and now the Russians are bombing it on their way in." As soon as Baba heard this, she packed a few things into a bundle and took me by the hand, and we walked to Franzensgasse. The apartment was empty, and the hat rack was gone. Except for a few small pieces of furniture there was nothing in the apartment. Within a few days we had a bed to sleep in, a large bed for the three of us in the bedroom, and a table with some chairs in the living room. My grandfather joined us, and we were all very happy. The bombing was still going on, and at night we could not turn on the lights in the apartment.

During the day Baba and I walked outside, disregarding the curfew hours. The war was not yet over, but there was a feeling of freedom. I think most Jews took off the yellow Star of David, and so did we. When we were in the apartment I was running around from room to room. The terracotta ovens were on in the early hours of the morning and in the evening. My grandfather brought wood and lit the ovens every day. I loved to stand with my back to the big oven in the living room and feel the warmth through my whole body. But most of all I loved to sit in the toilet room. This was a tiny room where I could be all by myself. Sitting on the toilet with the electrical light on seemed wonderful. I dreamed about some of the stories I knew, and I played imaginary games. The walls were white and clean, and in my imagination I filled them with pictures of fairies and animals. It was so good to be on my own and not being told off.

The neighbors in our building were all new. I heard Baba say that Dr. Segal was killed fighting in the Red Army and Mrs. Segal died in Transnistria of typhoid. The family living next door to us on the same floor were rich Jews who had friends in the Russian army, and they were always entertaining visitors who were very noisy. They had a little girl about my age, named Karin. She invited me to play with her. Baba would go out to find more things for our apartment, and I would stay with Karin. She had her own room with many toys, clothes, pictures, and books. I had never played with a girl before, and I did exactly what she told me to do. I could see that she enjoyed bossing me around, but I could not help it, and I just followed her like a shadow. Karin was the first person to offer me a piece of chocolate, and I knew I had to be nice to her.

One afternoon at the beginning of February 1944 when I was with Karin and her family and my grandparents were out, one of the other neighbors came running in and said, "Littika, Littika, come and see who just arrived!" My heart started pounding like a hammer and my feet became weak. Slowly I came out into the staircase. A beautiful woman with black hair and a heavy coat was standing there looking at me. I knew this was my mother, but I felt nothing. She picked me up in her arms and looked at me.

All the neighbors started yelling at me, "This is you mother; kiss her, hug her." But I was as stiff as a stone and completely speechless.

Then my mother said, "Leave her alone. She needs to get used to me." Luckily we were "saved" by my grandmother, who came running up the stairs. My mother put me down, and the two women hugged each other for a long time, with my grandmother sobbing. We all walked into the apartment, and the sirens went off again. "What do you do when the bombing starts?" my mother asked.

"Nothing much; we just stay here in the dark," my grandmother answered.

That night Baba and her daughter Frieda sat at the kitchen table and talked and talked. I was sitting next to them, resting my head in Baba's lap. I did not understand everything they said or what they meant, but I did hear Baba say, "What could I do? I had to give them everything otherwise they would have killed us. Nothing was left, and I had no money to feed the child or buy her clothes." I had a feeling that my mother was looking disapprovingly at Baba, as if she was blaming her for something. I was not very happy, and I did not know why. Then at some point my mother took out some money and put it on the table.

Just before daylight my mother packed a few pieces of food in her rucksack, gave me a quick kiss, and left. I did not see her again for a whole year.

I had been waiting for my mother for so long (two and a half years). All this time I had been thinking of her on the top of the suitcases on the cart that took her away from me. How could she leave me again? Did she care for me at all? Didn't she miss me at all, and didn't she want me now with her? I hugged my Baba with all my strength. Life continued as before, and soon I stopped thinking about my mother.

# Chapter Eight

# The Russians Are Here Again

The bombings had stopped, and the Russian soldiers filled our city. We were liberated from the Germans, but people did not seem happy. They all remembered the Russians from the first time they occupied our city, and they did not trust them. Baba and I went out a lot. The streets were dirty and smelled of sauerkraut (*kapusta*) and herring. I hated the smell.

The streetcars were functioning again, and we often went on them only to see some Russian soldier vomiting in the corner after having had too much alcohol to drink. Many young women in our building and in the neighborhood were complaining that the soldiers were harassing them.

Thin and hungry-looking Jews were returning from Transnistria to town, and Baba was waiting for her son Byumin to show up. She heard from someone that he was alive and spent the years in a labor camp. But then the terrible news arrived: On his way home from the camp Byumin had stopped to drink some water from a well, and a Romanian soldier hit him hard over the back with a big bottle. His lungs collapsed, and he died a few hours later.

For days Baba could not stop crying. She stayed in bed or sat on a chair in the living room, but she did not cook or go out. She looked completely broken down, and I did not know how to help. I just sat next to her and caressed her arms and face. My grandfather was sitting in his chair and sobbing. I had never seen him like this, and I felt very sorry for him. I kept thinking about my mother. Why wasn't she here with us? Why had she left again? Then one morning Baba got up and said, "God, how much suffering can there be for us! Haven't we had enough? But life must go on, and I must take care of you and feed you," she said, looking at me with deep concern. She got dressed and went shopping. We had a normal meal that day, and although Baba was still very sad, it looked as though we were going back to a normal life.

I had stopped asking her about my mother and why she left again. Baba had explained to me that Frieda had to leave to meet some important people and that because of the war there was a new border. She was now in Romania while we were in Russia, and it would take a while until we could join her where she was. Baba said, "We don't really want to stay in Russia, and as soon as possible we will follow her." I could not understand why, after we had been so happy to get back to our apartment on Franzensgasse, we would have to move again.

We received several postcards from Frieda from a city called Bucharest. She was doing well and waiting for us to join her. I did not think about her anymore, but I think I never forgave her for leaving me a second time. Years later in the summer of 2002, I was sitting in our apartment in Jerusalem, watching a program on TV. They showed an African woman from Angola who had not seen her son for four years since he got lost during the riots and fighting. Suddenly she was told that her son was found. He was twelve years old, and he was healthy and in good shape. They gave her a picture of him. The woman started to dance and laugh and cry. She was beyond herself with happiness. I was sitting there in my living room, and tears were running down my cheeks. I sixty-four years old and a grandmother by then, but the program took me back to my meeting with my mother when she returned from Transnistria, and it caused a dull pain in my chest. The questions were still burning in my brain: *Why wasn't she happy when she saw me? Was I in her way? Was I just an additional burden to deal with? How could she look at me after having been away for almost three years and be so indifferent? How could she leave me again?*

With the Russians in town, we were free to go everywhere. I walked with Baba to the Ring Platz and we saw a large golden star on top of a huge column. There was also a huge picture of Stalin. Many noisy Russian soldiers were everywhere, but we were not afraid, and we did not have to wear the yellow Star of David any more.

Baba had an idea, which she told me nothing about. She went to the Russian authorities and gave them the name of my father and all the information about him and asked them to find out what happened to him. Without saying anything she was waiting for an answer. She had hopes for his return, and she knew that we would get some money from the Russian army for my support, so that we could all eat. In the meantime she was taking on all kinds of jobs so that we could survive. She baked and sold some of her products, she sewed and mended clothes, and she mostly turned around collars of men's shirts and made them new-looking. And of course she always knitted, but that was for the family. She would undo old sweaters, and I would help her roll out the yarn, holding my arms stretched out for her to wrap the yarn around them. I loved to be with her during those times.

Food was now much more available than before, but meat was a very expensive product. The rumors were that when we bought meat, it was often horse meat that looked like beef. So another way to make money was to find a farmer who would bring large slabs of beef to town, and Baba would sell it to the neighbors from our kitchen.

One day we had half a cow on our kitchen table, and people kept coming to buy a kilo or a half-kilo of meat. Baba cut the pieces and named the price, and my grandfather weighed it on a scale with stones in one plate and the pieces of meat in the other. Since many people were coming and going, I was in charge of the door. I opened the door and said in German, "Please come into the kitchen."

One time I opened the door and I saw a very handsome Russian soldier in a heavy coat, standing and looking at me. He had a big smile on his face, and even his blue eyes were smiling. He said to me, "Littika, is it you? Is this my little daughter?"

I stood still for a moment, then ran to the kitchen to my Baba screaming, "Tata, is home; Tata is home!" He walked slowly through the corridor, limping a little.

# Chapter Nine

# Frieda

Frieda, my mother, had always been a very resourceful and clever woman. Members of the family used to say that Frieda was like a cat, *always landing on her feet*. On that gloomy October morning when she was sitting on the wagon full of sacks and suitcases, waiving "goodbye" to me, she was on her way to Transnistria, like many other Jews from the ghetto, on one of the early transports.

A number of wagons were moving slowly on the cobbled streets, toward the train station. Some people were walking with their small bags on their backs or in their hands. Everyone was quiet and bent down under the burden of fear and worry. Frieda, who was young and healthy and had prepared herself well for this ordeal, was in deep thought but not in despair. She trusted her own abilities to make things work for the best, and she also believed that she had a good chance of meeting my father.

The night before the deportation my grandfather had given her his old army boots, which fit her feet perfectly and were warm and comfortable. First he carefully opened a small slit in the sole, and Baba brought out some American dollars, which they stuck inside the sole and then fixed it so that no one would see and it would be safe. Then Baba sat most of the night and sewed Russian rubbles into the lining of the winter coat. She did such an incredible job that it was impossible to guess that something was hidden inside. She also managed to wrap some bread and cheese and fill a thermos with hot tea. All this Frieda took with her and felt that she was ready for the journey.

As they approached the train station, more and more groups of people, whole families, were huddling together and trying not to lose each other in the ever-growing crowds. The beautiful train station, built in the Austrian classical style, was still the same, but instead of being a place where people meet friends and family, where they depart to new places and exciting adventures, it was a place of fear, uncertainty, and despair. It was obvious to all these people wearing the yellow stars on their coats that they were about to face catastrophe, although they had no idea what it really meant.

Frieda spotted Oncle Herman Rosenbaum, Baba's youngest brother, his wife Kutza, and their son Freddy, who was about eighteen years old. She had always liked them. Kutza was one of the most educated women in the family: she had *Matura* from Vienna and later studied pharmacology. Frieda grabbed her things and ran to them. They were happy to see her, and the four decided to stick together.

As Frieda and the Rosenbaums embraced each other, Romanian and German soldiers were screaming and pushing people on to the train. Frieda looked up at the train. She could not believe it—they were asking them to climb into empty wagons used to transport animals. Before she knew it, she was pushed up and had to make an effort to hold on to her suitcase and rucksack and locate Oncle Herman and his family. Finally she managed to move over toward them inside the wagon, and they were all standing clinging to the wall of the wagon, where there was a thin slit of air and light. When the big heavy doors were shut, they realized how fortunate they were to be standing near this only source of air.

The first few hours went by with people standing or sitting close to each other. It was particularly hard for children and old people. Many children were crying, and the old were groaning and sobbing. It was hard to think clearly. People were taking out bits of food that they had carried with them. They were eating in silence, each person to himself. A thought flashed through Frieda's mind: *How wise it was to leave Littika with my mother. She will take care of her—what would I have done with her here?* After a while, the situation became very tense because everybody needed to go to the toilet. There were some pots that were passed around, each person relieved him or herself, and then the content was thrown out through a small opening in the door. Still the stench became insufferable, and it was hard to breathe. Frieda was glued to the wall and the slit of air. Her thoughts were focused: *I must survive this terrible situation, no matter what.* After many hours of traveling, no one knew exactly how many, the train stopped, and they all had to get out to the screams of the Romanian and German soldiers. It was cold and gloomy outside. No one knew exactly where they were, but they knew it was somewhere in the Ukraine.

The word went around that it was Ataki near the river Dniester. Suddenly there were loud screams from the Germans to start walking toward the river. This large body of people started moving slowly in deep mud as rain was starting again. The old people could not carry their packages, and the children could not walk in the deep mud. Many people just fell and could not get up again. Frieda had her rucksack on her back and a suitcase with many of my father's clothes in her hand. She walked as fast as she could in order to get over this ordeal. The Rosenbaums kept close to her. When they reached the river people were hoisted unto small boats aimed to cross the river to the other side, to Moghilev. The Rosenbaums boarded a small boat and called Frieda to join them. She was unable to balance herself with the large suitcase in her hand, so she asked a German soldier to help her with the suitcase. He looked at her with an evil grin, grabbed the suitcase, and threw it on the ground while pushing her on. All her cherished things lay now in the mud. That was a sobering moment for her. She quickly got on the boat and later noticed that some Ukrainian children rushed to collect the scattered things. Her sobering was translated into a decision: *These people are out to kill us. I have to take care of myself. I must survive and do the best I can.* Later she said about the incident, "That was the moment when I stopped being naïve, and I stopped relying on others—all my life I have fenced for myself. I don't owe anybody anything." These were words that she often repeated to herself and to others.

As the boat reached Moghilev it began to snow, and it got freezing cold. Frieda had her large shawl, which Baba had knitted for her, tight around her body. Her boots were lifesavers since they had a warm lining inside and they were sturdy enough to withstand the mud and the water. As they stepped out of the boat they could hear the screams of the German and Romanian soldiers, and they were pushed onto the bank like animals. At the same time there was sobbing and quiet crying all around. People had fallen into the Dniester and drowned before they reached Moghilev; others had given up and remained in the mud only to be beaten to death by the soldiers. Again the old and the children were the first to pay with their lives.

Uncle Herman had spoken to a few important Jews he knew, and he learned that the best thing for them would be to leave Moghilev right away. Around the huddled, shabby-looking, and completely exhausted Jews who had just come off the boats, there was a ring of small carriages and carts with horses and Ukrainian drivers. They were standing there, grinning and waiting. Uncle Herman went up to one of them and asked him to take them to Murafa, which he had heard was a nice village, not too close to Moghilev. The Rosenbaums had some Russian rubbles with them, and they paid him right away, so the three of them and Frieda mounted the carriage. They were huddled together, but two more people could join, so they saw a couple they knew and asked them to join them. The six of them were sitting in the open cart, covered with some old blankets, with the snow falling on them all the way to Murafa. Snow was better than rain since they did not get drenched in humidity. They were all silent during the journey except that some stomachs began to grumble—they had not eaten since they got off the train and had no food left. The journey lasted most of the night, and they reached Murafa early in the morning. As the cart was pulling up in the center of the little village, not far from the beautiful Catholic church, other carts with more people seemed to follow. They all got out and started jumping up and down to warm up the legs and feet and feel alive again. They knew that they were the lucky ones because Murafa was already known as a cleaner and better place than all the other ghettoes in Transnistria.

As they were standing there in the cold, some Romanian soldiers came and told them to find a place to sleep and report the next morning for work. Frieda noticed a Ukrainian woman standing nearby. She had a smile on her face, and she was holding a large barrel with hot soup. People came up to her, and she sold them a cup of soup for a few *kopeys*. The Rosenbaums also sipped some soup, and then Frieda whispered something in the woman's ear in her broken Ukrainian and the woman smiled and nodded. They waited till she finished selling her soup, and the four of them, Uncle Herman, his wife Kutza, Freddy, and Frieda, followed the woman. She took them to her house where she offered them a small room with some mattresses on the floor. The room had two windows, one of which was broken, and the cold wind blew through it bitterly. There was an outhouse in the yard not too far away. They agreed on the sum of money they would pay her for a week and then began to settle down. Uncle Herman used the back of a suitcase to block the broken window. They were all completely exhausted but also very pleased to be able to finally sleep in a lying position. They all knew that so far they had been very lucky. They also realized that every penny was important in the survival effort. My mother put her boots under her head and thought that she would delay using that money as long as she could. She did, however, get a few rubbles out of the coat for the next few days.

This was the first night in Murafa, sometime in late October 1941. Frieda remained in Murafa nearly two and a half years. She stayed with the Rosenbaums in the same little room for almost a year. The landlady was a lonely woman whose husband and sons were away at war, and she lived on the income from the rent.

The morning after the arrival to Murafa, all the Jews were called to the small central square, and they were sent out to a variety of jobs of hard labor. The deported Jews were standing huddled together while local Ukrainians who needed workers looked them over. Among them was the director of the small Murafa hospital, which was now providing health care to the Romanian and German armies. He spotted Frieda in the crowd; she was a beautiful woman who looked young and healthy and had a certain air of confidence. He approached her and spoke first Romanian and then German to her. As soon as he realized that she was German-speaking, he smiled and said, "I think I have some work for you at the hospital." And this is how, lucky again, Frieda got a job inside, out of the cold, where she could also get a meal and wash up after work. At the beginning she was asked to wash floors and clean the washrooms. Hard work for a young woman, but she was strong and healthy and worked fast. Soon the chief physician, a Ukrainian woman, suggested that she take care of her room and area of work, and a certain friendship developed between them. Frieda felt rather privileged.

Late in the evenings when Frieda came home to the Rosenbaums, she always brought something to eat—bread or potatoes. Most of the people in Murafa were suffering of hunger. The typical food was potato peelings cooked as a soup. Especially in winter, there were no vegetables and no dairy foods. Only people who had good connections and a little money could get some eggs now and then and perhaps some butter. Frieda soon made a lot of connections. Through the Ukrainian physician she met the commandant of the Murafa Ghetto. He was a German and liked Frieda right away. He always had a joke or a story for her when he came to the hospital. Once he told her, "If you ever need help or are in trouble, come to my office. I will instruct the soldiers to let you in."

Frieda soon found out where one could get clothes, food, pieces of furniture, and other things. Most of the young men were sent to hard labor camps from which they never returned. The families who had young sons were in constant fear that their sons would be taken away. Many of them approached Frieda, since word got around that she spoke to the commandant. They gave her watches, bracelets, gold coins, and diamonds to give the commandant and make sure that their son would not be taken. She used to go to the office, sit in front of the commandant, and put the valuables on the table. Then she would mention the name of the young man and leave the room. Most of the time, she managed to save these men for whom she paid in family gold and jewelry. It was always a miracle how these miserable people had managed to hide valuables in their clothes, corsets, coats, shoes, pots, and pans.

One day Frieda had an exciting encounter with Tanya, the physician for whom she was working at the hospital. Tanya called her into her room and told her secretly that she was getting married but she had no wedding dress. Frieda's eyes sparkled—*this was her opportunity to help her superior.* She found a Ukrainian woman who had some white linen and another one who was a seamstress. Within a week the physician had a very beautiful wedding dress, and she always remembered that favor. Frieda now had a friend among the leaders of the camp.

Many of the Jews adored Frieda for her abilities and unusual skills; others hated her. The committees established for the Jews, the local religious leaders, and many others felt that she was getting in their way. The religious leaders wanted people to come to them when in trouble. They were against those individual deals and private arrangements that Frieda was good at. Frieda usually ignored them, and when confronted she always said: "Let them do the best they can for the community. I rely on no one but myself. So, I have my own connections and my own way of doing things."

One day Mrs. Druckman, who used to be a neighbor of my grandparents, approached Frieda. Their son was thirty years old, and he had worked in a small local shoe factory. Now there was talk that they would send him away to a labor camp. Could Frieda save him? Mrs. Druckman put a beautiful gold bracelet in her hand. Frieda went once again to the commandant. This time he was angry. He said that these people are needed for the war effort and they should do their duty. As usual she put the bracelet on the table and mentioned the name quietly. Then she walked out. She was not sure that this time it would work. She went straight to the Druckmans. She told them that she was not sure that she had convinced the commandant. There was a lot of crying and unhappiness, but the parents and young Poldy Druckman were very grateful to her. They asked her to stay the night with them and wait together for the morning.

Poldy and Frieda sat all night and talked. Frieda told him about Willy, who was probably dead, and her little daughter, who stayed behind in Czernowitz. A special understanding and bond developed between them. By the morning he was holding her hand and caressing it gently. Suddenly they could hear the screams of the soldiers. They were hoisting out another group of young men to send to the labor camp, beyond the Bug. Frieda and Poldy sat embraced looking at the door and waiting for the pounding, but it never came. Once again she had managed to save a young man. When everything was quiet again the Druckmans and Frieda embraced and kissed and were the happiest people in the world. In recognition and gratefulness Mrs. Druckman offered Frieda to come and live with them. The conditions were slightly better than what they had at the Rosenbaums, and she finally accepted the generous offer.

For the next year and a half Frieda lived with the Druckmans. The closeness, the anguish, and the young hearts soon led to a love story. Frieda and Poldy became lovers, and their love gave them great comfort in those difficult times. They were both working hard and surviving on the meager meals that the Druckmans could put together, but under the danger of being sent over the Bug or dying of the local diseases, they had each other and that gave them hope for the future.

Frieda and Poldy knew that they were fortunate to be in Murafa. Other places in Transnistria were much worse. In Murafa, like everywhere else, many people died of hunger and cold and many were sent over the Bug. Yet sanitation and basic conditions were better than in other places, and the terrible typhus fever and typhoid epidemic did not spread as fast. Most of the survivors had places were they worked daily, although without pay, yet receiving shelter for their work. Food although scarce could be bought or traded for from the local Ukrainian farmers, and many of the Jews had brought some money and valuables with them. Frieda used most of the rubbles she had in her coat, but she kept the dollars in her boot until the very end.

As time went by news from the front reached the small ghettoes in Transnistria. The German defeat at Stalingrad gave everybody new hope. Yet the Germans continued to kill Jews, sending them over the Bug or to labor camps or just shooting people who were not in line with the regulations.

Poldy had two close friends who were eager to try and escape from Transnistria. They felt that staying to the end might cost them their lives, and in the winter when the Germans were themselves weak and unhappy and the Romanians were too lazy to keep close enough guard, they should try to escape. The idea was for the four—Poldy, his two friends, and Frieda—to escape together. Frieda was the only woman in the group, but they all had high regard for her abilities and practical thinking, and they felt that she was an asset to them.

While the Germans and the Romanian soldiers were drinking and celebrating the New Year at the beginning of January 1944, the four took off. For this occasion Frieda got out the dollars from her boot and changed most of them to rubbles. It was a small fortune, which would last her for a while. With small rucksacks on their back, the four started first on foot, then with a cart, and then on a truck, making their way towards Czernowitz, which was at the time under heavy bombardment from the Germans who were leaving and the Russians who were approaching. At each point they paid their way and were not asked questions by anyone. The farmers were all aware of the fact that Germany was losing the war, and even if they guessed that these were Jews escaping from the "lager" of Transnistria, they only cared about the money.

When the four entered Czernowitz on a cold afternoon in January, they decided each to look for some of their family members who had stayed in town and try to spend the night with them. But the agreement was to meet the next morning and continue their route going south towards Bucharest. That is why Frieda spent only that night with Baba and me, left some of her money, and went on the next morning. She had a lover, she had a group of close friends, the war was almost over, and she was hoping to build a new life for herself. She was certain that my father had died in the war. And where was I in those plans? She probably did not know where I would fit in, and therefore it seemed best to leave me with Baba, who had taken such good care of me and who was now safe in the old apartment on Franzensgasse.

# Chapter Ten

# Willy

My father, Willy, was recruited to the Red Army in March 1941. He underwent army training at the large military camp located in the outskirts of Rosh where my mother Frieda and I used to visit him every Sunday. We were both looking forward to these visits, and we often brought him something nice to eat and sometimes my mother brought him some books to read. He always liked to read and to tell stories. The long walk from our apartment to Rosh was pleasant because we stopped in Schiller's park, and I had time to run around and play. We were supposed to visit my father, as usual, on Sunday the twenty-second of June as well, but history had a big surprise in store for us.

On Saturday June 21, 1941, the Ukrainian and the Jewish young soldiers were playing soccer and having their usual little quarrels and competitions. It was a sunny afternoon, and they were all out in the field. Willy, as always, was in the center. By now all the soldiers knew that he was strong and in great physical shape. Being a good gymnast, he always did his exercises on the bars. Suddenly the teasing of the Ukrainians became a confrontation with the Jews. Anti-Semitic slogans were being thrown around, and the atmosphere became quite heated. One of the

Ukrainian guys walked up to the Jewish "leader" and said, "You Jews talk a lot, but deep down you are cowards. Let's see if one of you can take on our strong guy, Sasha. We dare you to find a Jew who can stand up to him."

Sasha was six feet tall and was a heavy man with a furious temper. The Jews looked at him and asked for time to consult. They moved away, and in a small circle, whispering in German, they expressed their concern to each other. "What do we do now? If we don't confront Sasha, they will never leave us in peace. Who can stand up to him?"

Then one of the guys shouted, "Willy, you are much smaller than Sasha, but you are the strongest among us. What do you say?"

Willy looked at him with a big smile. "Of course. It will be just like David, and Goliath and you know the end of that story." Willy looked anxiously at Sasha, but he knew that he could not let his friends down. Their honor depended on him.

As soon as Willy agreed to the fight all the soldiers began cheering, and they all ran to the open training field. There they stood in a wide circle and allowed for Sasha and Willy to position themselves in the center. Willy and Sasha began wrestling. Sasha was strong, but Willy was quick and knew how to dodge the furious blows. The Ukrainians were cheering their hero while the Jews were standing quietly in disbelief. After a while they too began to scream, "Willy, Willy!" This gave my father added energy, and suddenly he embraced Sasha in the middle of this body and lifted him up in the air. Sasha screamed and fell to the ground, defeated, but this time Willy did not dodge fast enough, and the big Ukrainian landed on his left leg. The whole crowd of soldiers went wild screaming, "Willy, Willy!" and Sasha walked away in disgrace. As the Jewish young men came to pick Willy up and cheer for him, they realized that he was in terrific pain. His leg was broken at the ankle.

Willy was taken to the infirmary and his leg was fixed to a plank. The doctor was to come in the morning and decide what to do. In the meantime they brought him a bottle of vodka to quiet down the pain and to cheer him up. Although he had never had strong alcohol before he drank a full cup and felt better. All his Jewish friends sat around him beaming with delight. It felt so good to overcome those nasty Ukrainian swines. And for a brief moment, Willy was the hero of the unit.

As night fell and the vodka intoxicated him, Willy managed to fall asleep in spite of the pain. At around five in the morning all hell broke loose, all of a sudden. The whole area was bombarded, and shells began to fly through the air. Panic struck the whole Russian army camp. Soon the orders came in, and it was decided to evacuate the whole camp immediately. All the soldiers, including the whole Jewish group from Czernowitz, were put on a train and sent deep into Russia—all except Willy, who was sent with the infirmary to a military hospital in the town of Gorky, far away from the fast-advancing front.

The shelling and the bombing became stronger, and as daylight broke, the train with the Jewish soldiers was hit and completely destroyed. All the passengers were killed, and the Jewish young men from Czernowitz were among them. A single Jewish man managed to survive, and he got back to the city and informed everybody that the Jewish group was gone, but nobody knew that Willy had not been on that train.

What happened on Sunday June 22 was the beginning of "Operation Barbarossa," the German codename for the invasion of the Soviet Union. The German attack caught the Russian army by surprise. The speed and the force of the attack completely disrupted the Russian defense plans. Fast retreat was imminent.

Willy reached a large army camp near the town of Gorky. This was away from the front, and the soldiers were training and preparing for a brutal war with the advancing German army. He was brought to the military hospital, which was much better equipped than anything they had in Rosh. His leg was placed in a cast, and he was given a pair of wooden crutches. He had no idea what happened to his friends, and everybody around him spoke only Russian. His Russian was not very good, but he soon discovered the Russian library on the camp, and so he began to read in Russian—first magazines and then books. His Russian gradually improved, and he made some new friends among the guys who came to the infirmary. He had no news, of course, from his family. He wrote some letters to Frieda but the letters never reached their destination, and soon he gave up hope. He knew that the Germans burned everything in sight and killed all the Jews on their way. There was no chance that his family would survive.

The infirmary was run by a woman doctor, who was stern and very focused on her work. But she soon took interest in the young handsome man, who was struggling with the Russian language. She noticed that he could read Latin words easily, and even before his leg healed she asked him to work for her in the infirmary. So, Willy became the *feltcher*. He wrote down the names of the different medications and kept a log of incoming and outgoing medications on a daily basis. His handwriting was beautiful, and his boss was very pleased. She began to like him and trusted him with all the equipment and the medication at the infirmary. By the end of October 1941 his leg was healed, but he still limped and needed to walk with a cane. So he continued working in the infirmary. These were Willy's best months in the army. He did not have to stay out in the bitter cold for hours on end as the other soldiers did, and he had a lot of time to read. The food in the infirmary was better than what the regular soldiers got, and most of the time he could sleep through the night.

Willy's Russian friends liked him a lot. He would usually let them have his portion of vodka, and sometimes when one was desperate for a drink he would let them sip some medical alcohol in the infirmary. He soon learned many Russian songs and every evening the soldiers, half drunk and half sober would ask him to sing for them. The months passed, and the war was still far away.

What happened to Czernowitz? What happened to his wife and daughter whom he left behind and with whom he had no contact now? He had no information about anything except for the fact that the battles in the Ukraine had been fierce. Yet everybody knew that the German army was stuck in the Russian winter and could not advance in the manner they had hoped for.

The German army's huge losses and hardships in Russia since "Operation Barbarossa" in June 1941 did not dismay Hitler. As spring of 1942 approached it became clear that the Germans would restart the *blitzkrieg*. Willy realized that he would not be able to stay forever in the infirmary, and being young and healthy they would soon send him to the front. In May 1942 he was assigned to an artillery unit and began intensive training. The easy days were over.

In the artillery unit the training was intensive. The soldiers were woken up at four o'clock in the morning. They were given a large bowl of hot soup with ham in it, and then they were sent out for training until the sun set. First Willy could not touch the heavy soup in the morning, but soon he realized that there was nothing else to eat all day and he learned to "enjoy" the morning soup.

In June 1942 the Germans launched a new offensive. They were advancing quickly towards Stalingrad, and units from the Gorky camp were sent as reinforcement to the army defending Stalingrad. By October 1942 Willy's artillery unit was sent toward Stalingrad. First his unit stayed in a little shack at a distance from the front where the Germans and the Russians were fighting at very close range. As the weeks passed by, it got colder and colder. The soldiers just sat huddled together in the shack, and in the evening they drank their ration of vodka and sang songs. Then in December they were moved closer to the outskirts of the city of Stalingrad. The fighting was fierce, and they could see how the city had become a heap of rubble.

The Russian soldiers buried themselves deep into the trenches surrounding the city, with branches of trees above them. The snow had covered everything and in a way was keeping them warm in their dug-in holes. As they sat this way, taking turns at firing the artillery at the Germans they could hear the Germans in their own trenches or in spaces created by the collapsed buildings. The Germans would often address the Russian soldiers in German over loudspeakers: "You brave Russian soldiers, Germany is not your enemy. Surrender and we will make sure that you have a much better life than here under the Bolshevik regime."

The other soldiers always asked Willy to translate the German words for them, and then they would scream back, "We will never surrender! We are going to kill you one by one!" Sometimes the Germans would turn on some German songs, and Willy enjoyed listening and humming along.

Every day more and more Russians and more and more Germans were killed by bombs, shrapnel, and snipers from both sides. But the Germans' real enemies were the lice and the cold. They were not used to these terrible conditions, and many of them just collapsed. One day Willy heard that the Germans deserted a position close to him. He waited until everything was quiet, placed his helmet on top of his rifle as if he was standing at his post, and he crawled out into the deserted German position. As he had hoped, there was a field shower there and some German newspapers. He even found a towel, some soap, and clean underwear. What a delight! He could have a real shower after all these weeks in the same clothes. He took a long time enjoying the water and the feeling of freedom and cleanliness. He forgot all about the constant shelling and bombing all around him, and after he got dressed and all freshened up, he sat down to read a few German papers that were lying around. It was so good to go through the German written words. It took him back to days that he had almost forgotten. Finally he gave up the comforts of the German post and crawled carefully back to his position. He looked at his helmet, which was still in its place but it had a hole in the center. "Another narrow escape!" he said to himself.

After a few more days Willy's unit was allowed to return to its shack away from the front to rest for a few days. As they were sitting there, one evening all hell broke loose. There was a terrible artillery barrage from the Germans, and the shack got a direct hit. When everything calmed down, some of the soldiers lay dead, some were wounded, and Willy just remained in the same sitting position. Suddenly he felt a very sharp pain in the area where he had broken his left leg during the fight with Sasha, the big Ukrainian guy. He looked at his leg in the heavy winter boot, but he could see nothing. He tried to lift the leg, but the excruciating pain caused him to faint.

Willy woke up from his swoon to find himself in an ambulance rushing him to the field hospital. The pain in his leg was terrible; he looked down and he saw that the boot and the sock had been removed. His leg was swollen, and he could see a small wound on each side of his ankle in perfect symmetry. The feltcher sitting next to him smiled: "Yes, isn't it funny—the shrapnel went in from one side and came out on the other side."

In the hospital the situation was very bad. Hundreds of beds were lined up next to each other with moaning soldiers who were attended by a few nurses. Willy was brought into the operating area. Two surgeons examined him. They worked fast and made quick decisions. They agreed that he needed an immediate operation, but the older one said, "We must amputate," while the younger surgeon kept saying, "He is so young; let us try to save his leg." With these sentences ringing in his ears Willy succumbed to the gas mask. A few hours later he awoke with a terrifying thought—*My leg is gone*. He reached out with his hand toward the injured leg and felt the cold cast. He clamed down: A cast meant that the leg was saved.

The recovery was slow, but in comparison to all the terrible injuries around him, Willy knew he was very lucky. He soon began to walk around with crutches and to tell the soldiers nice stories and sing songs with them. The important thing was that he would not have to go back to Stalingrad. For him, the war was over.

In February 1943, two months after Willy had been wounded, the Russians were able to free Stalingrad. Willy was now walking with a cane and feeling back to normal. The officer in charge of discharging injured soldiers from the hospital invited him for an interview. He said, "Well, you have done your duty soldier, so now we are going to release you. What would you like to do?"

Willy smiled to himself at this statement. He knew that veterans, or anybody for that matter, were not free to travel or do anything they liked in the Soviet Union. One had to accept what was being suggested, otherwise there could be trouble. Furthermore, the war was still going on all across the Western Front. Still he decided to address the officer with a personal request.

Willy had heard about the new metro, which was being built in Moscow, so he asked to be sent there so he could use his skills in marble works. The officer smiled and gave him a note and instructions to take the train to a small village farther east. Obviously his request was not being taken into account. Willy had no choice but to follow the instructions.

He arrived in the village early afternoon and went directly to the officer *nachalnik* in charge. The man looked at him and his papers and told him to sit down and wait. Soon he came back with an older, stern-looking woman who stretched out her hand and introduced herself. "I am the principal of the local high school," she said, "and we need teachers. What can you teach?"

Willy thought for a moment and then said, "Perhaps drawing?"

The woman smiled and said, "All right, but you also speak German, and we want you to teach our young boys German." Then she explained to him that the village was in a very difficult situation; there were no men to do the work in the fields and in the workshops. The women were doing the best they could, but there was no food and no money. He would not be paid a salary, but he will be given wood for heating. The wood could serve as rent for room and board in one of the local homes.

Just as she showed him where to pick up a load of wood a small and smiling young woman came up to him. "I have a nice room for you, and I can cook your meals." She had a friendly smile and a twinkle in her dark eyes, so Willy followed her. She introduced herself as Natasha.

Natasha led Willy to her small home. It was a farmhouse with a yard around it and a few chickens wandering around. Inside there was a large living room and a kitchen with a stove, which Natasha lit right away with the wood that Willy brought. The place became warm and cozy. Natasha lit some candles and an oil lamp. There was no bathroom or toilet in the house, but there was an outhouse in the backyard. She made some soup for Willy and cut him a big piece of black heavy bread. She sat and looked at him as he ate. He asked her whether anyone else lived in the house, and she explained that her husband was killed in the battles of Stalingrad and they had no children, so she was living alone in the house.

Natasha showed Willy his room with a comfortable bed and a large down cover. A pair of warm pajamas, which had belonged to her husband, was lying on the bed. There was a small closet in which he could keep his things. He looked at her and said, "This is really very nice. I think that I will be very comfortable here, but there is one thing I need, and that is a hot bath" She smiled shyly and ran out, coming back with a big wooden pail, large enough for a person to sit in. She fetched some water from the well outside and filled several large pots and placed them on the stove. In no time the pail was full with hot and soapy water and some towels next to it. Natasha told Willy he could have his hot bath and she would be in her room.

Willy took off his heavy uniform and slipped into the hot water. What a pleasure—he could relax and enjoy the feeling of warmth throughout his whole body. When he was done he put on the pajamas and crawled into bed. He felt like a new person. Simple things in life could be so wonderful. He was not going to think about the war at all. With a smile on his face he fell asleep.

A few hours later Willy was suddenly awake. Natasha, dressed in a thin nightgown had crawled into his bed and rolled up next to him. He had not been with a woman for a long time. He had almost forgotten the feeling. "Life will be good here," he whispered to himself in German.

The days went by pleasantly. In the morning Willy taught German and drawing. He did not enjoy it very much. His students were arrogant and did not study on their own. He had to keep them busy and interested during the lessons since they were not keen on studying. Every morning they came in reporting the latest news about the war advances. The Russians were constantly pushing the German army back. Many of his students were thinking of joining the army soon.

After his teaching he took long walks in the woods near the village. His foot still hurt, but it was getting better. Then in the evening he would spend time with Natasha. She wanted very much to please him, and she did everything for him. She was a good cook and a very warm and loving person. He felt happy and thought that he may spend a long time in this small village. He was quite certain that his family in Czernowitz had been killed, and so there was no rush to go back there.

A whole year went by this way. The Russian army was victorious on all fronts. More and more cities were being liberated, and in April 1944 Willy heard that Czernowitz and Bukovina were liberated and North Bukovina returned to the Soviet Union.

Should he make an effort to get permission to go see his hometown? From what he heard on the news every day he was sure that his family had been killed. He saw no reason to leave Natasha and his comfortable life.

Then one day at the end of the summer of 1944, a Red Army representative came by and asked to speak to Willy. They were sitting in the living room, and Natasha served some hot tea from the samovar. The representative looked around and sighed deeply. "I see you are living comfortably here as a couple. Well, I am sorry, but I have some bad news for you. Here is a letter from your family in Czernowtzy" (the Russian pronunciation). Natasha's hands started to tremble, and she could not hold the cup of tea. Willy took the letter quietly and read through it without saying a word. It was the letter from my Baba who was telling him that I was alive and well, living with her and Grandpa in our apartment on Franzensgasse, and that my mother had survived the concentration camp and fled to Bucharest. His heart was beating fast—they survived, his wife and child were alive but in separate places. Could he go back now and reunite his family? Could he leave Natasha and forget his present life?

Willy was very quite for a while, then he looked up at Natasha and said, "Well, my family survived the war. We must talk." The army representative left after sending an empathetic glance at Natasha. As soon as he left, she ran to Willy sobbing. He tried to quiet her down and said, "I am not leaving right away, but I think I must go and see them, perhaps in a few weeks." This was typical of Willy: "Don't make a difficult decision right away; let it happen slowly!"

One day in October 1944, Willy was standing at the entrance to the apartment on Franzensgasse, looking at his little daughter.

# Chapter Eleven

# My Father's Great Disappointment

The first few days with my father back home were painful. He looked at me in amazement and expressed his great disappointment. "Where is that sweet little girl I left when I went away with the army? She was so bright and happy and full of life." Then he looked at Baba. "I cannot believe that this pale, sad-looking, and scrawny girl is Littika. Nothing reminds me of her." He touched my thin braided hair with what I thought was definite disgust. He looked at my clothes and said that we must buy some new clothes that fit a six year old.

Finally after he got over the initial shock, he began telling his stories about the war and his injuries. Everybody was amazed to hear how he was wounded twice in exactly the same spot on his left ankle. Many people came to meet him and treated him like a hero. I tried to enjoy these events, but most of the time I was worried that if I said anything I would disappoint him even more, and so I was quiet.

The winter was cold, and I finally had some warm clothes that Baba and my father bought for me. I could leave the house for walks with my father, and once he even took me to a movie. It was the first time I saw a movie and I was very excited, but I still felt shy and uneasy with my father. I did not know how he expected me to behave, and I was too shy to tell him how I felt. I couldn't tell him that I was hungry or cold. I just sat next to him and listened when he spoke to me. Then the most terrible thing happened. As the movie started and I was enthralled in the story (it was in Russian which I could not understand, but I could tell what was happening from the pictures), I suddenly needed to go to the toilet most urgently. There was no way I would say anything about it to my father, so I held my breath and tried to hold it in. I felt I was going to burst, and before I knew it warm urine was running down my legs and on the seat. It was very dark in the theatre, and the only sound came from the movie. Nobody heard or saw what happened to me, least of all my father sitting next to me. I shifted my sitting position a little and relaxed. What a relief! I was terrified that he would find out, but at the same time I felt good. Soon the warm feeling turned into ice cold. My legs were freezing and my skirt became stiff, but I paid no attention to it. The movie was long, and gradually I got used to the fact that I was a little wet. When the movie ended we got up to leave. I put on my long warm coat, which covered everything. My father did not say anything, and neither did I. We went out into the street. Now I was freezing again. We got on the streetcar and went home. When I entered our apartment I ran to Baba and told her what happened. I never found out whether my father even noticed my terrible plight.

One day my father received a letter with many stamps on it. He opened it quickly and read the letter several times. Then he called Baba and asked her to sit down. I was sitting quietly in my corner, where I made it a habit to spend my time when I did not want to be in my father's way. In a quiet and low voice he began to tell Baba about Natasha. I was straining to understand what he was saying. *Who was Natasha? Why was she important? Why did my Baba look so shocked, and why did she place her hand on her mouth in such pain?*

When he finished his story he suddenly said in a much louder voice, "Well, Natasha is arriving tomorrow, and she will stay here with me for several days. I would like you and Leizer (my grandfather) to move to the living room with Littika, and I want to sleep with Natasha in the bedroom. Baba was so shocked that she said nothing. Then Willy put on his coat and left.

Baba had not moved from the couch where she was sitting. I got up and rolled up against her. She embraced me and sighed: "*Mein shatz* we have some problems to solve together." Then she got up, and she was really angry. "How can he ask me to give him the bedroom to sleep in with this Russian woman? This is also Frieda's apartment! How can I allow this to happen?" She wrung her hands and walked back and forth. Then she called my grandfather from the bedroom and told him the whole story. He just sat there and said nothing. She finished her part by saying, "Look what this war has done to all of us. People are crazy!" And with this she walked into the bedroom and started to strip the bed. I ran after her to help her.

I did not know what to say to all this, so I kept very silent. The next morning Natasha arrived. As soon as she hugged and kissed Willy she walked over to me and hugged me too. She took out a little package and told me in Russian that this was for me and I should open it. There was a necklace inside made of delicate red beads. She put it around my neck, and I felt happy. This was the first real present I received since the turquoise earrings, which I was still wearing. Natasha seemed so nice and friendly, and I liked her. Baba said a few words of hospitality and brought some tea and cookies that she had baked. Then my father went into the bedroom with Natasha, and they spent most of the time there for almost three whole days. On the fourth morning they came out together, and I could see that Natasha had been crying. She came over and hugged me again and said something in Russian that I did not understand, and they both left. About an hour later Willy came back and told Baba, "You don't have to worry. Natasha left, and she will never come back again." I think my grandmother was very pleased, but I was a little sad.

A few days after Natasha left my father said that we were invited for lunch with Tante Regina. I really did not want to go, but he asked Baba to dress me up and comb my hair nicely, and the two of us walked all the way to Regina and Yossel's apartment. Yossel was at work, and we sat at the table with Regina, Nora, and Mina and another cousin, an older man whom I did not know. Mina, the youngest of the three sisters, was dressed up in a beautiful dark blue dress, and she had a long string of pearls around her neck, tied in a knot on her chest. Her hair was combed nicely into a bun on the top of her head. She had lipstick on her lips and looked very beautiful. I remembered her from the time I stayed with them in the apartment and could not believe that this was the same person. She was now friendly and happy and talked and giggled most of the time. After lunch she walked over to Willy and hugged his neck from behind laughingly. What was she up to? She was even nice to me. I looked at my father. He seemed to be very pleased with himself. Then they all asked him to sing some songs. My father stood up and began singing; first a few German songs, then an Italian song, and finally some Russian songs. He had a beautiful tenor, and everybody applauded him. I was very proud of my father although I had felt uncomfortable most of the time during this visit. Regina had not said one word to me and neither did Nora. Were they still angry at me for running to the door to wait for my mother when I had stayed with them?

Finally the visit was over. Before we left Mina hugged my father and gave him a big kiss. As we walked into the street Willy said, "We are not far from the Volksgarten, and since the weather is nice let's take a walk" I was very happy that he wanted to walk with me, and I smiled happily.

As we began walking along the more hidden paths of the park he suddenly said: "Littika, do you remember the movie we saw together?" My heart stopped beating—had he noticed my accident? Is he going to scold me now? But he smiled and then said, "Do you remember, the pilot's wife in the movie who waited for him to come back from the war? He lost both his legs, but she remained loyal to him, and she was happy to see him come back to her. But your mother Frieda is very different. I went to war, I was wounded, and she did not wait for me at all. In fact she has a lover with whom she lives in Bucharest now. This is not how a wife should behave, and we are not going to call her "Mama" anymore. From today she is simply Frieda." I was shocked, and I felt my cheeks burning. I did not know what to say, but I knew that I would never call my mother Frieda. She was my "mama" forever.

In the evening we came home. Baba waited for me. She and my grandfather had moved back to the bedroom. She took me into bed with her and wanted me to tell her everything that happened at Regina's. When I told her she started sighing. "You see, Littika, Mina has always been jealous of your mother, and now she wants to take your father away from Frieda. That is why she put on such a show today. But we must not let this happen. Your father must get back to Frieda, and the three of you should be a family again." I listened to her, and I decided not to tell her what Willy said during our walk in the Volksgarten. In fact I promised myself never to tell it to anyone. I knew my Baba was right and that things would work out somehow.

# Chapter Twelve

# Learning to Play with Children My Age

I was used to spending all my time with adults. The only games I played were games that I could play with them, such as dominoes or simple card games. These were available in the house even when there were no toys, and the adults were often happy to play with me. Adults usually let me win and gave me encouragement. There was no real competition.

Children who were my age frightened me a little. Karin, my neighbor, seemed so sure of herself and so strong, and I continued to follow her orders without a word. I knew that this was not the best way to behave with her, but I could not do anything else. Still I liked being with her and playing with her toys. This was a new world, and I was curious. One day I followed her to the backyard of our building. There were other children there, playing with stones, wheels, and other broken or used utensils. I was following Karin as usual. I could see that she was whispering to an older boy, looking at me, and laughing. I realized that they were making fun of me, but I decided to ignore it. Then as we were running after a kitten, the boy pushed me and I fell on some broken glass, which cut my knees and my two hands. Blood was coming out of all the cuts, and I ran up the stairs crying and sobbing straight to my grandmother. For a few days I avoided the children in my building and spent most of my time with Baba, but my soul and mind wanted to be out there with the others. My father looked at me and laughed: "You are like an injured soldier back from war."

About a month after my father's arrival, Karin and her family moved away. Again I was spending too much time with my grandmother. I joined her on daily trips to various parts of our little town. One day we saw a large caricature on the wall. It showed Hitler with his head under an ax, and there was a big question mark around him. I asked my Baba what this drawing meant, and she explained that everybody thinks that Hitler died but they never found his body so they are not really sure. *He must be dead*, I thought to myself. *God would not let him live after he had done so much harm in this world.*

One morning my grandmother woke me up earlier than usual and said, "Today you are going to go to the kindergarten. I bought you some new clothes, and I will take you there." I was shocked and worried but also very pleased. I knew children my age were supposed to go to school and to kindergarten, and I was happy to be like everybody else. We arrived at an old building with a large yard with tall trees. Near each tree there was a wooden table and some chairs. Boys were running around the yard and screaming in Russian. I recognized the language, but I only knew a few words in Russian. I clung to my grandmother. We walked into the building, and a big Russian woman smiled at us. She said that her name was Katia and immediately put a little white apron on me. My grandmother gave me a hurried kiss and left.

Katia spoke to me in Russian, but I did not understand what she said. She pointed to some toys in a corner, and I began to play by myself. After a while a big girl with a runny nose sat next to me, and we played without talking. Every now and then she would say something to me in Russian, but I only shrugged and continued playing. I could not understand how she continued playing without being bothered by her runny nose. I took out my handkerchief and wiped my own nose.

Then we all went out into the yard and sat near the tables. Each of us got a glass of milk and a piece of black bread. Some of the boys were fighting with each other. Some came running near the girls, pulling their braids or taking their bread away. Katia was too busy to see everybody. Somehow they looked at me and left me alone. I probably looked very small and miserable and dumb since I said nothing all day. I noticed though that the girls who were annoyed by the boys shouted back at them and said, "*Ia razkaju tebia*." I soon realized that this meant, "I will tell on you." I tried to remember the phrase in case I would need it some day. We ate lunch together and played some more, and finally Baba came to pick me up. The kindergarten was not far from our apartment, and we walked together in silence.

I went to kindergarten for a whole week. Every day it got worse. The boys began to tease me and hit me. I kept using the phrase "*Ia razkaju tebia*" very often, but it did not help much. I still could not understand what the girls were saying, and some of the older girls tried to protect me from the boys, but they too pushed me around and made me play games I hated. They smelled badly, and they looked dirty. I felt like crying all the time, but I decided not to show my weakness. Katia never really talked to me since she realized that I didn't understand her anyway. Things seemed pretty bad for me. Then one morning when Baba was getting me ready to go to the kindergarten I began to cry, and I told her how miserable I was there and that I did not want to go. She listened to me carefully and after a while said, "You know what? You don't have to go anymore. You can stay home with me." I was sitting on the bed, and suddenly I felt very sad. A big hollow place opened up in my tummy.

*Why doesn't Baba make me go to kindergarten? I know I should go, but I don't have the strength to force myself to do it. She should make me go! She is responsible for me. My father said that he did not care if I went to kindergarten or stayed home, so he won't help me. The only one who can help me is Baba and she, out of her kindness and love, decided to give in to my childish revolt. What is going to happen to me?*

I remained on the bed sobbing to myself for a long time. I was worried that I would never go to school and I would never learn to read. Then I came to a decision, and I made a promise to myself: *I will become strong and make my own decisions. I will never stop something in the middle. I must learn to force myself to do things that I am supposed to do.* I decided that the next day I would force myself to go to the kindergarten and tell my Baba not to listen to my complaints. Later that day my face became red and swollen. Soon a lot of small blisters developed around my mouth. My grandmother got very worried and called the doctor.

He looked at me and said, "I think I know what this is, but she has got a very bad case. She will need to stay in bed for a while and put some ointment on the blisters. They will grow and look even worse before they get better." I ended up staying in bed for a long time. The doctor came every few days and put other medications on my face. I was suffering terribly. But eventually I got better, and I never went back to the kindergarten.

Now again I spent a lot of time with the grown up people in our family. I loved to play by myself in the yard, and I used to look for cigarette butts for my grandfather. He used to open up the buds and fill a little tin with the tobacco. Sometimes he would take a thin sheet of paper, the size of a cigarette, fill it with some tobacco from his tin, and roll up a cigarette, which he then smoked. When he was in a good mood he would let me roll him a cigarette.

My Russian remained limited to the one phrase I used in the kindergarten, but my decision to fend for myself in the future became a personal resolution for life.

# Chapter Thirteen

# Leaving Czernowitz

One day Baba sat me down in her lap and said, "Littika, the time has come for you and your father to go to Bucharest and join your mother. You three must be a family again. And you, Littika, have to help your parents to get together and to want to live together again. You are very important to them." I listened carefully, and I felt like Baba had just put a big bag on my back. I was not sure what I was supposed to do, but I remembered my walk with my father in the public garden, and I was happy he wanted to go and meet my mother.

I suddenly realized that I would have to leave my grandmother without knowing when I might see her again. I got very worried and truly frightened, but I decided not to say anything so as not to add more worries to my Baba's concerns. I knew that this was the right thing to do and that I had to try my best to follow Baba's instructions. I squeezed her shoulders, I buried my head in her chest, and the tears ran down my cheeks noiselessly.

It was not possible for a veteran of the Red Army to leave the Soviet Union and go to another country like Romania. So Baba had managed to buy some forged papers and passports for my father, myself, and two other young women (supposedly my father's sisters). We ended up meeting two strange women who were supposed to travel with us on our common papers. We all had to practice our new names and our new family relations. It was very strange, and my father explained to me that we had nothing in common with these two women but we must travel on the passports together only until we cross the border into Romania.

The day arrived when we had to leave. Baba and my grandfather hugged me and kissed me. Baba said to me, as if reading my mind, "Don't worry, Littika. We will follow you soon." A cart drawn by a little horse waited for us on a street corner not far from us. My father was carrying a large potato sack with clothes in it and a small suitcase. The cart took all of us—the two women, my father, and myself—to the border at a town called Siret. It was early in the afternoon, and everybody was hoping to be on the other side of the border before night fell. There was tension and silence in our little cart. Nobody spoke, and nobody looked at me. I felt a little lonely, but I was also very excited. This was my first trip outside Czernowitz. I did not realize that we were going into another country, another language, and another culture. It was early in June of 1945, and the war had finally ended even in Germany. Everybody was hoping for a better life and a new beginning.

When we finally arrived at the border we saw a lot of carts waiting in line. "The border has been closed for several days, and you will all have to wait here," the policeman told us. "You can all sleep in the school building over there."

We all took our packages and walked over to the school. There was a huge hall there, and each family found a little spot for themselves to sleep and huddle together. The two women disappeared in the crowd. My father and I found a place between two other families, and my father put his coat on the floor and the sack of clothes and said to me, "Here we will sleep tonight." He gave me a piece of home-baked bread that Baba had given us and walked away. It seemed like hours went by before I saw him again. In the meantime I spoke a little to the people on our right. They had a little girl smaller than me, and we began playing together with some pieces of string. They also gave me a hard boiled egg and a piece of cake to eat. On our left there was an older couple, who seemed very quiet and sad. Later I found out that the woman's name was Tea, and her daughter had died in Transnistria.

Late that evening, when most people were asleep, my father came and lay down next to me. He asked me if I was hungry; I told him that the neighbors had given me some food, and he smiled and said goodnight. The next morning we all woke up early, packed our things, and waited to continue our trip. Finally a policeman opened the door and walked in. "The border will remain closed for a few more days," he announced. There was a loud murmur in the crowd. Then he said, "You can stay and sleep here in this hall, or you can find rooms in the homes of the villagers."

My father and I, and our fictitious family, decided to rent two small rooms in a farmer's house where we stayed for a whole week until we were allowed to continue our journey. On the day that the border opened there seemed to be hundreds of people walking toward the border check point as well as a few carts drawn by tired horses. "Our family," Tea and her husband, and a few other women whom I did not know shared a small cart. All our packages were on the cart while we were walking next to it. Suddenly Tea took me aside and said to me as if I was a grown up, "You know that at the border they will search our bodies for money and valuables, and we are not allowed to take anything with us. But you are a child, and they won't search you. So I want to put my money in your jacket, and you will give it back to me after we cross the border." She pushed a little bundle of notes into my shirt. As I was wearing a training suit with and elastic band at the bottom, the bundle just stayed put above the band.

Suddenly all the other women came to me and said, "We want you to hold our money as well." Before I knew it I was stuffed with small bundles of money in my pants and my top, and I was too shy to say anything. Also deep down I felt good that suddenly everybody was nice to me. My father seemed to know nothing about these deals, and I never told him anything.

As we approached the border all the men were taken to one side and the women to another side. Tea said to me, "Pretend that you are sick, and stay on the cart." But a policewoman came and told me to walk together with the women. I walked next to these strange women and felt my face hot and burning.

I told myself, "I am going to try and pass the check point slowly without looking at the policewomen. If they catch me and undress me I will pretend to cry, and I will say that I don't know whose money this is." But, although I was frightened and worried I felt important. I had a mission to carry out, and some people depended on me. Not my father though, and I was sorry he did not know anything about this mission, yet I would not tell him. Years later, when I told him the story, he could not believe it.

As we approached the checkpoint I saw Tea being stripped naked. She was white and trembling, and I thought she might collapse any minute. Then some other women went through the checking. I looked at their faces and became more frightened myself. As I came closer to the policewomen who were checking the women, I slowly walked behind them, and suddenly I was on the other side. Nobody stopped me, nobody looked at me—I had crossed the border!

All the women were directed to a large hall where families reunited and found their personal belongings. Soon the various women came to me, and each one fetched out her little bundle of money. Some hugged me and said, "Good girl!" Others just took the money and expressed a big sigh, "Thank God." In a few minutes I was with my father again, and the ordeal was behind us.

My father was holding the big potato sack when he noticed that one of the seams had opened and some Russian rubles were peaking out. He began to laugh. "Your Baba did not sew our money too well, but we crossed the border and nobody noticed. Now we are free and we don't need our fictitious family anymore. Let's go and find a way to travel to Bucharest."

Eventually we found ourselves on an open truck going to Bucharest. We were part of a large group of people, and we ended up sitting next to each other for a whole week. The truck stopped several times on the way, and we slept in schools and other public places. A week later we arrived in Bucharest where Frieda was waiting for us at the Spatzirers, cousins on my mother's side.

# Chapter Fourteen

# Can We Be a Family Again?

I was very excited and very anxious about the meeting with my mother. When they opened the door at the Spatzierers I saw a room full of people I did not know. My mother came over to the door and greeted us. She was more beautiful than I remembered. She looked at me and at my father for a long while and then she said, "Come in; everybody is waiting for you." There were no hugs or kisses, just looks and half smiles. I had no idea how my parents felt toward each other; I could not tell anything from their behavior. As for myself, I felt that I was not really important at the moment and so I kept very quiet, but I was happy to hear that everybody was speaking German.

The other people in the room were much more excited than the three of us. Somebody raised a small glass of wine and said, "It is amazing to look at the three of you here with us. We thought that you, Willy, were killed in the war, and for a while we thought that Frieda died in Transnistria, and we knew nothing of you, Littika. And here you are together again." Everybody drank and ate, and some people came to me and hugged me and offered me all kinds of food. I could not really eat anything or think about anything. I was thinking of Baba. What would she want me to do? How should I behave?

In the evening all the visitors left. Tante Mali took me to a tiny room with a bed and a chair in it and said that I could sleep there. It was the first time in my life that I slept in a room by myself. She told my parents that since they needed to talk to each other quietly, she was giving them the room next to mine. I was given a pair of pajamas, and the light was turned off in my tiny room. I lay quietly on my bed, and then I heard my parents talking in the other room. I crept quietly to the door and stuck my ear to the keyhole. Now I could hear them very clearly. I stayed like this for hours until the first signs of morning came through the blinds of the tiny window. My parents talked all this time. They told each other about the years they were apart. That was how I learned all the facts about them. At the end I heard my father say, "Well we have both been through a lot. I think that we are very lucky that we are alive and healthy and still young enough to begin again. We should become a family again for the sake of our 'kind' (child)." Did he mean me? Was I a good reason for becoming a family again? Where is my Baba? I could ask her what all this means.

Exhausted, we all fell asleep for a few hours, me in my tiny room and my parents next door. Then I woke up very hungry. I walked into the living room, and my parents both smiled at me and hugged me and kissed me in front of the Sparzirers. They said solemnly, "We decided to try to live together as a family. We will all need to make an effort to get used to one another again." They explained that they would be looking for a place to live and for a place to open a workshop for tombstones in Bucharest. (My mother had already checked for suitable areas). In the meantime we could stay with the Spazierers for a few more days. After breakfast they looked happy and refreshed. They bid me goodbye and left.

Tante Mali hugged me and said, "You are very quiet, Littika, but you should be happy today. Now you have a family again, and your parents have survived the war and are together again." I understood what she meant, but I felt a little confused. Then she called her son Freddy, a nice boy my age. I had been so anxious about my parents when my father and I arrived the night before that I hardly noticed him. He spoke to me in German and showed me toys and books in his room. It was nice to play with someone my age. I began to feel happier, although I missed my Baba terribly. I wanted to tell her everything as I always used to.

Every night my parents would come home late and they would tell the Spatzirers of the events of the day. They asked me how I spent the day but did not really pay too much attention to me. Then one day, they came home from their daily search with good news. "We found a suitable place for a small workshop near the Jewish cemetery—at the outskirts of the town. We also have the opportunity to rent a room for the three of us in a large estate, which is about a forty minute walk from the workshop. We can move in tomorrow." This is how the welcoming stay at the Spatzierers ended and a new chapter in our life began. I felt that this was a good beginning.

# Chapter Fifteen

# The First Day of School

Early in the morning we arrived at the *Budui* estate, far away from the center of the city. My mother explained to me that this was a noble Romanian family, and we should behave well and keep to ourselves as much as possible. We would have just one room to sleep in and we would use their kitchen in order to cook some basic meals for ourselves. They had a large farm with pigs and hens and a huge orchard with all kinds of fruit trees. This could be a paradise for all of us, but especially for me.

It was a nice summer day. Mrs. Budui, a small woman with a very stern face, met us and showed us into our room. She said that in a month or two they would be able to offer us another small room so I could have my own room. In the meantime we had to sleep together, my parents in a double bed and me on a small mattress on the floor. As soon as we put our few things down in the small room I asked my parents if I could go outside and look around. I had learned a little Romanian from my cousin Freddy, and I felt that I could manage on my on. I also realized that Mrs. Budui was a very well-educated lady and she knew a little German.

Mrs. Budui had come to Romania from Russia, where she had belonged to a noble family. She and her son Yuri had to flee after the Soviet Revolution. They found refuge in Romania where she met Mr. Budui from a Romanian noble family. After the war things were hard for them too, and therefore they had to rent out one of their rooms in order to make some money this way. But food on the farm was in abundance. Mrs. Budui took me under her wing and decided to teach me how to behave the proper way. I was eager to learn.

In front of the house there was a huge nut tree with a table around it. In the summer the Buduis used to have lunch there. When her son and daughter-in-law would visit, Mrs. Budui would serve them special dishes under the tree. I liked to sit at a distance, minding my own business and watching the Buduis. It was like watching a movie. I noticed how Mrs. Budui used to set the table: plates, napkins, and silverware. Once she told me that one should know how to set a table properly, and if I wanted to learn she would teach me. I was fascinated since in Baba's house we never bothered to set the table like that. Once I felt totally surprised when I saw Yuri eat a big slice of watermelon using a fork and knife. I promised myself that I would learn to eat this way too.

I spent the days walking around in the orchard, learning to feed the hens and the pigs, and observing the Buduis. I wanted to learn everything from them. My parents would come home late at night after a long day's work and bring some salami and bread, and we used to eat in our room with the gas lamp lighting the table. Although the estate was big and the Buduis seemed to be rich, they had no electricity or running water in their home, but there was a telephone in their living room, which never rang. The toilet was a terrible outhouse in the yard, which stank so badly that I always went in there with a kerchief tied around my nose and mouth. I could not understand how such rich people could live like that, but I soon got used to it. On Saturdays we would be allowed to use the kitchen for our weekly bath. This meant filling up a large pail with warm water and taking a bath in it. My mother used to wash me in this little tub, and this way she spent some time with me. During the weekly bath she talked to me, sang some songs, and made me feel very happy. Getting into clean clothes after a bath was the best feeling in the world. After we all took our baths we used to sit in our room, and both my mother and father sang songs in German or Russian and told stories.

At night they would get into their bed, and I would lie on my little mattress. I often could not fall asleep, but I heard them whisper to each other, "Oh, she must be asleep by now," and I pretended to sleep. I could hear them chuckle and whisper and breathing very fast and their bed would creek. I did not know what was happening, but I decided that they were probably having fun because when it stopped they used a lot of nice words to each other and they kissed a lot. So whatever was going on must have been good. I fell asleep feeling happy.

The summer days at the Buduis were passing by slowly. I played with Elena, the maid's daughter, who was a little older than me, and I learned a lot of words and expressions in Romanian from her. My parents started talking about school. I was supposed to go to a Romanian public school in the fall, and I was seven and a half years old but did not know how to read and write. My father decided to teach me. He brought home a little blackboard and some chalk, and he began teaching me letters in Romanian. He taught me ten letters by writing them down and sounding them out, and then I was supposed to copy each letter. The next day he decided to test my knowledge of the letters he had taught me, and I knew most of them but could not distinguish between "e" and "f." He asked me again and again, and as he was getting more annoyed with me I became more confused. Finally he screamed at me that I was stupid, and he smacked me. His ring left a scratch on my cheek and the smack left a big scar in my heart. I could not stop crying for a long time, and I ended up sobbing uncontrollably. Finally my mother came and asked what was going on. My father said, "I tried to teach her the letters of the alphabet, but she is too dumb to learn."

My mother looked angry, and she said to him, "You have no patience, and you cannot teach. Just leave her alone. She will learn how to read and write in school. We are going to put her in first grade. Most children in first grade are a year younger, but I am sure that there are other kids her age, who missed the first year because of the war. They will all learn how to read and write." Listening to her I realized that I was older than other kids in first grade and that I should learn how to read as soon as possible, but there was nothing I could do on my own.

One day my mother came home with a few new dresses for me. "Tomorrow is the first day of school. I have been there today, and I think you will like it. Tomorrow morning I will take you there." The following morning she combed my long hair into braids and dressed me in a lovely blue dress. On top of it I wore a stripped frock, which was the uniform. I took my little blackboard and the chalk, and we walked together. First we crossed the field and reached the street on which my parents' workshop was. We waved to my father and continued walking for another hour till we reached the school. My mother took me to the classroom and told the teacher my name, then she left.

The teacher, a large woman with a bun of dark hair, smiled at us and told us to sit up straight. Then she called our names, and we were supposed to stand up and say "present." I could understand most of what she said since my Romanian had been improving. She began to teach us the first two letters of the alphabet and some basic math. Her explanations seemed very easy, and I knew everything that she was teaching. I felt good. I noticed that some of the other children did not understand very well. Then we went out for the break. There was a big yard, and I walked slowly with my apple and my piece of bread. I had no one to talk to. Three girls walked behind me. One of them said, pointing at me, "You see this girl—she is Jewish." And she spat at the floor.

The other two laughed, and then one of them said, "I thought Jews looked even worse than this." I felt my face flush, and I threw my apple and bread away. How did they know I was

Jewish? What did they know about me? I decided to ignore such evil girls, but I also knew that I would not tell anyone that I was Jewish unless I had to.

By the end of the day I walked out of the school with the other children. I passed through the gate and began walking home. I knew the way and wasn't scared. Suddenly I saw my mother walking toward me. She had a big smile on her face. "Littika, you know how to walk home by yourself?"

"Yes," I told her. "Tomorrow I can go to school by myself, and I can come home by myself." She seemed very pleased, and she hugged me and kissed me.

Every morning I walked for an hour and a half to school and an hour and a half back. On the way back from school I stopped at the workshop and stayed there for a while. There were usually a lot of people, speaking Yiddish, German, and Romanian. These were Jews who came to buy a tombstone for a Jewish grave. My mother was busy showing them all kinds of pieces of marble and granite. I liked to spend time in the workshop.

After several weeks at school I made a few friends. I became particularly friendly with a girl called Marina. She came from a little village that was even further than the Budui estate. In the morning I used to meet her in the big field, and we walked together. She was usually barefoot and walked on stones and shrubbery as if nothing even hurt her. She was a shy and quiet little girl, and I was happy that I could help her.

When I came back from school and stopped at the workshop, I often used to watch my father color the engraved letters on the tombstones. The letters were Roman letters and Hebrew letters, and he used to color them in black or gold. Soon I learned how to do that, and I enjoyed helping my father.

One day the teacher at school made a special announcement: "A very important group of inspectors are coming to visit our school on Sunday. Although this is usually our day off, this coming Sunday we are going to have classes. But you can come later and leave earlier. We will only have two hours of class, and the inspectors will watch us learn. You don't have to wear your school uniform. You can come dressed in your best clothes." Each of us received a note for our parents to explain the importance of that day.

When Sunday finally arrived, I wore my new blue dress, and my mother put two big blue ribbons in my hair. It was a beautiful sunny autumn day, and I was very excited. Marina told me that she could not come on Sunday so I walked by myself. The school was decorated with a lot of flags; many of them were red flags. Our teacher was dressed nicely, and she was particularly friendly. She met each of us at the door and walked us to a seat (not our regular seats). She put me in the first row, and I felt my legs tremble. In the back of the room three strange men and two women were sitting and watching us. The lesson began. The teacher repeated things that we had learned and then suddenly she called me to the board. I walked up hesitantly as she said, "Melica (that is how the Romanians always called me instead of Melitta), write the following sentence on the board: 'Un cuc pe un nuc.'" I knew the meaning of the sentence (a cuckoo bird on a nut tree), and I knew how to write it.

*If I can only stop trembling*, I thought. Slowly and carefully I wrote the sentence between the red lines on the blackboard. When I finished the strangers in the back of the room applauded. My face burned, and I quickly sat down in my seat. I thought that the teacher must like me if she made me write in front of the whole class and the important visitors. The lesson ended, and I wanted to leave and run home. Many of the other kids were picked up by their parents, but I knew how to go home by myself.

I walked all the way to the big field. It was sunny, in the early afternoon of a Sunday. I could hear the buzzing of bees and the mooing of cows in the distance, but I was all alone in the big field. Suddenly out of nowhere, four boys, bigger than me, began walking right behind me. I walked faster, not looking back. One of them came nearer and asked me what my name was. I whispered an answer. Another asked me where I was coming from. And I said, "From school." They began laughing loudly, and suddenly they surrounded me.

I tried to avoid them and continued walking, but they grabbed me and didn't let me move. "Come with us," one of them said. "We will have fun."

I got scared, and I said, "No!" My parents are waiting for me." Then they pushed me down to the ground and began touching my body. I knew that I was in real danger, and I had to fight them back. *I will not allow them to do anything to me*, I thought, and with all my strength I began hitting and punching them one after the other, and they cursed me but drew back a little. Then I screamed at the top of my voice—a scream so loud and fierce that I was not sure it had come out of my own throat.

Suddenly one of them said, "We'd better get lost." He kicked me, and they all ran away. I straightened my dress and my hair and continued my walk home. By the time I reached the Budui estate my legs stopped trembling and my breath was back to normal. *Never will I let anyone harm me. I will fight back until I die*, I thought to myself and joined my parents in the yard. I told them everything about the strange school day but not a word about the incident with the boys. Then I went into the orchard and found a branch that I could put in my school bag. If anything like that ever happened again I would hit them so hard that their eyes would pop out.

At the end of the school year my mother was invited to join me for the end of the year celebration. A lot of children and parents were crowded in the large hall. The principal was standing in the middle and calling out names from the higher grades. I did not quite understand what was going on, and neither did my mother. Suddenly the principal called out my name. My mother pushed me forward toward the principal, who grabbed me smilingly and lifted me up on a chair next to her. "Third prize in first grade," she shouted and then handed me a certificate. I was shocked and so was my mother. *I was the third best student in class.* I could not believe it.

My mother looked very pleased, and together we walked home. "I didn't know you were such a good student," she said. "Let's go home and tell Tata." From that day on, everybody expected me to be a good student.

# Chapter Sixteen

# Life under the Communists

We stayed at the Buduis until the end of the summer, and then we moved to a little house on the main street leading to my parents' workshop. From here I would have to walk only one hour to school rather than one and a half hours. Marina still came by my house and waited for me every morning at the gate to our yard. The house was small with two rooms and a dark hall, which served as a kitchen. Here too the toilet was an outhouse. But the most wonderful place was the yard with lots of trees and bushes.

There was electricity in the two rooms in the house, but there was no light in the kitchen, and we had to use a gas lamp there. There was no running water, but there was a well in the yard, and I soon learned to fetch water from the well. In the winter my father would buy a lot of wood in order to heat the big terracotta oven in the living room. He taught me how to cut the wood in small pieces, and so my chores were to fetch water and cut wood. I also learned to cut vegetables for a salad and cook potatoes. Before my parents came home to eat I could always prepare a few things that my mother told me. If I failed to do what she said, she got very angry, and sometimes she hit me and slapped my face very hard. I knew she was basically good to me, but I also thought that she did not love me very much.

The most disgusting chore I had to do was buy a live fish, carry it home squiggling in the net, and then try to kill it and clean it. I hated to kill the fish so I used to put it down on the board, throw a wooden hammer at it, and run away. When I came back and the fish was motionless, I was relieved; if it still moved on the board I repeated the action of throwing the hammer at it and running away. This procedure took a long time, and sometimes I failed to finish cleaning the fish by the time my mother returned, and that was good reason for a spanking. She wanted me to clean the fish, take the inside parts out, and cut it in slices ready for her to cook it as quickly as possible. To this day I dislike cleaning fish.

At the beginning of the following school year I went back to school by myself with Marina. We had the same teacher. She was nice to me and put me in a good seat. Suddenly a lot of kids were friendly toward me, and during the break I had lots of friends to play with. It seemed that they forgot I was Jewish.

One day in second grade the teacher came to class with teary eyes. She said, "Today our king Michai abdicated. Open your books to the page where we have his picture, and tear out the page. Also tear out the page of the queen mother. From now on we are a republic." We tore the pages in silence. Most of us did not know exactly what this procedure meant, but my parents explained to me that now we were part of the Communist world. A few weeks later there were elections. Hundreds of people filled the streets. The Communist party was the strongest and they were elected by over 90% of the population. My parents told me that we had to be very careful and pretend that we liked the communists.

At the end of the second grade I received the first prize for being the best student in my class. My Romanian was perfect now, and I was good in math, so I began the third grade as the star student in the class. I was soon elected to be on the class committee, and I became a young pioneer wearing the red kerchief. In the third grade we began learning Russian. This became my favorite subject, and my Russian teacher loved me. Whenever she had to leave class she would ask me to conduct the lesson in her place. I was feeling great. At the end of that year I was selected to represent the whole school in a writing competition of the whole city of Bucharest. I received the third prize, and the school was very proud of me. The principal invited me to her office and gave me a special certificate.

One day when I came home from school my parents were very excited. They had received a letter from my father's sister and her family in Los Angeles, the Buchbergs. Through the Red Cross they had managed to locate us and get our address. We soon began to receive care packages with clothes and all kinds of delicious foods such as chocolate and coffee. But my parents said that we should not talk about it since some of our neighbors might be envious.

Then one morning when my father went particularly early to work, four men knocked on our gate. My mother opened the gate and asked them to come into the house. They said that they were from the investigation office and they wanted to search our house to see if we had hidden gold or dollars. I could see that my mother was quite frightened, but she said, "Please search wherever you like." They overturned the whole house, the cabinets, the beds, the various cases, and anything that could be opened. They had a hard time looking in the kitchen, which was dark and terribly disorganized. Finally after two hours of searching, they said that they found nothing, and they left.

I did not go to school that day. My mother and I sat for a long time and looked at the overturned drawers and the clothes and papers that lay all over the small house. Finally we got to work to put everything back. When my father came back my mother said, "Tomorrow I will register as a member of the

Communist Party. That is the only way I can protect us from such searches."

As a party member my mother soon became a leader. She read a lot of the propaganda pamphlets, and she prepared lectures and sat for hours to repeat the key sentences that she needed to present at the meetings. One of the women leaders, a Jewish woman, became her close friend and would come several times during the week to prepare the meetings with her. Her name was Valentina. I disliked Valentina because she always asked me to do something for her, and she never spoke nicely to me. My mother said we should be very careful with Valentina because she could be quite dangerous. She could report us to the party for the smallest offence.

One day toward the end of the winter, my mother came home with three fresh cucumbers. We all loved salads, and the cucumber season was just beginning. They were still very expensive, but we could afford to pay the price since my father's business was doing very well. As my mother was cutting the cucumbers we saw Valentina at the gate. In a frenzy my mother hid the cucumbers and the peelings under some pots in the kitchen and with a towel tried to disperse the smell. She looked at me sternly and said, "Valentina must not know that we have cucumbers. She will report me to the party for having money to buy cucumbers." I knew I had to shut up.

As soon as Valentina walked into the house she said, "Wow, I can smell cucumbers. Who can afford cucumbers today?"

My mother laughed and said, "Valentina you are imagining things. Indeed, who can afford cucumbers?" They sat and talked for a while.

Still Valentina was sniffing around and saying, "I am sure I smelled something like cucumbers." She looked at me, but I did not even blush. I just looked back at her. Finally Valentina left, and we laughed loudly and finished cutting up the cucumbers. Nothing ever tasted that good!

One day when I was in third grade we received a wonderful letter from Czernowitz. My grandparents were coming to Bucharest. My parents went out immediately to find an apartment for them, not far from where we lived. When they finally arrived I was beyond myself with happiness. I stayed with them and slept in their apartment for several days. But soon I realized that they had aged considerably during the two years since we had left Czernowitz. Neither of them could work and earn money and they depended upon my parents who helped them, but I could see that my grandmother was not happy with this situation.

We received nice letters from the family in Palestine, and my uncle Srul encouraged my grandparents to try join him and his family on the kibbutz. This was the period of the British Mandate in Palestine, and Jewish immigration was illegal. Many of the immigrants who arrived in Palestine by boat where either sent to Cyprus where they were held in a camp or sent back to Europe. Still many Jews tried to get papers to leave Romania. So my grandparents decided that they would go to Palestine. My grandmother offered to take me with them and later my parents would join, but after a lot of discussion my mother said that now that we were one family we should not separate again. I was very happy to hear her say that, and I felt that perhaps I was wrong and that she really loved me.

My grandparents eventually ended up in Cyprus where they lived for a year in a retention camp, and only after the State of Israel was established in 1948, they joined their son Srul in Israel on the kibbutz. For us life went on quite happily in Romania, except for the weekly tension and stress that my mother had before her presentations at the Communist Party.

I was growing up and developing very fast. Suddenly I was the tallest student in my class. Then one day I discovered some blood on my underpants. I got very frightened since I had no idea what that meant. I was sure that I had hurt myself or done something wrong. I did see my mother using some rags that were stained with blood, but I was sure it had something to do with older women. My mother must have noticed something, and so she and my father confronted me and she said in an anxious voice: "Are you bleeding?" I did not answer but stood there in a complete stupor. She came over and lifted my skirt in front of my father: I just wanted to die. This was so embarrassing and shameful. What had I done wrong? What was happening to me? They left me alone and quietly talked to each other. Then my father told me to go with him into the big yard: He had to talk to me. We sat under the tree, and he tried to explain to me what the bleeding was all about and that from now on I would have it every month. I listened and said nothing. I needed to think about this bombshell. I had never heard about it, and my grandmother was gone. Who would explain things to me? None of my girl friends in class were as developed as I was. My breasts were still small, and I could hide them in my loose uniform. I wanted my mother to tell me things, but she simply showed me the rags that she was using and said that I needed to wash them in cold water right after I used them. I promised myself that if I ever had daughters I would prepare them for this stage in life more carefully and more lovingly. For a while I was so discouraged that I even thought of suicide, but then I began to realize that this was the normal way of life, and I learned to accept it.

As time went on, my parents began to consider leaving for Israel. However, everything had to be done in great secrecy. We were particularly afraid that the party would find out about our plans and that Valentina would report our intentions of leaving. Eventually she realized that my parents were trying to get ready to leave. She informed the party leaders, and at one of the weekly meetings my mother was reprimanded, disgraced, and thrown out of the party as an "unwanted element." At this point it was clear that we had to finish everything very fast and get out.

Since my parents had money, they paid the full price of the tickets and services to the Joint, and we were given tickets for the boat to Israel. In three days they sold the furniture, closed the business, packed the forty kilos that we were allowed to take with us, and we had a taxi take us to the train station. I did not say goodbye to any of my friends, and I did not get the report card for the end of the fifth grade.

# Chapter Seventeen

# A Long Journey to a New Country

We arrived at the train station just before dusk. There were other families like ourselves, carrying small suitcases and small bags with sandwiches. They looked tense and suspicious. My mother kept whispering under her breath, "Let us go already. I just hope that someone hasn't followed us and will take us off the train" (she meant the communists or her party members who might find something wrong with her or our family and send us away to an unknown place). To me her worries seemed unfounded but still, it made my heart shrink.

We all boarded the train from Bucharest to Constanza, where we were supposed to board the ship to Palestine. It was the beginning of June 1950. It seemed that everybody on the train was Jewish and going to Palestine. A lot of people huddled into the small compartments and the long corridors of the train. We had a compartment with a couple a little older than my parents. The wife was sitting near the window very quietly while the husband was running around and talking excitedly to everybody. He introduced himself and his wife to my parents and myself. He pressed my hand with a big smile and a wink in his eye. There was another older woman who was dozing off near the door.

The train started moving. My parents sat down and let out a big sigh of relief. They were very tired and wanted to rest. I, on the other hand, was much too excited to sit in one place. I felt that we were about to embark on a new and exciting life, and I did not want to miss a moment. So I went to the window to watch the forests pass by and listen to the sound of the train. This was my first train ride, and it was wonderful. I was breathing in the cool night air, and I was happy. Suddenly I felt someone standing very close to me. It was the neighbor in our compartment. He hugged me and touched my breasts. I was furious; I wiggled out of his embrace and went into the compartment. My parents seemed asleep. As I was standing in the middle of the compartment he walked in and began telling me about the cities and the places we were passing by. Again he came close to me and put his two hands on my breasts. I did not know what to do. I did not want to cause a scandal, and yet I could not stand it. For the rest of the night I tried to avoid him, and he came back again, touching my breasts every so often, ignoring the people around us.

Finally it was dawn and we arrived at the harbor. Thank God, with the crowds of people pouring out of the train we lost our neighbors for ever. Although the ship was supposed to leave in the evening, we all boarded the ship. Since my parents had paid the full price for their tickets we received a lovely cabin with three beds and a sink. My parents said that they would stay in the cabin, but I could walk around on the deck. My mother was still worried that someone could come and take us off the ship.

I was fascinated by all the preparations and the activities that were going on all day involving the crew of the ship, and I spent most of the time watching all this. It was a dream come true. For years I had been reading adventure stories about explorers in Africa and the discovery of America, and I had always wanted to travel by ship. Now my excitement had no limits. I spoke very little to other travelers on the ship, but each person expressed their expectations for the new country. One person said, "We are going to an arid land, all sand and camels and deserts."

Another person said, "We are going to live in a Jewish State, and you should start behaving Jewish and not smoke on the Sabbath." I listened to all these people, but in my heart I had my own vision of the new country: proud, hard-working people, who were trying to be free and independent. I very much wanted to be like them.

In the evening the ship was finally ready to leave port. Everybody crowded on the deck, and there was no room to move. We had a wonderful cabin because we paid for our own tickets. Most of the other people had received tickets from the Jewish Agency, and they slept in crowded quarters on the lower deck. When we felt completely at sea my mother hugged me, and my father and said, "That is it. Nobody can stop us now." We went into our cabin and ate some of the food we brought. Suddenly my mother said quietly to my father, "You know that on the train there was this man in our cabin who kept touching Littika's breasts. I am glad we haven't seen him again." As I heard this I choked on my last bite. I couldn't believe the fact that she saw this behavior and said nothing. She actually could have protected me from this character, but she did nothing. I left the cabin, and for a long time I stood on the deck watching the black waves and gazing into the dark horizon. I felt very alone and wanted to see my Baba again.

I loved the sailing on the ship, first the Black Sea with its dark waters for a whole day and a night, and then gradually we were gliding through the Bosforus straights early in the morning and into the blue sea of Marmara. Then the ship stopped right in front of Istanbul, or what we called Constantinopol. We were all amazed at the beauty of this city: the green slopes, the minarets and the mosques, and the red roofs of many buildings. It was breathtaking, and I sat down in a quiet place on the deck and wrote a three-stanza poem in my personal diary. My language was Romanian, of course, since this language was now closest to my heart and I was literate in it.

Finally after sailing for two more days and nights, one morning just before dawn there was a lot of noise and excitement on the deck. We were approaching the port of Haifa. I was standing there, watching the sunrise and expecting to see the sands and the camels that people were talking about. Soon Haifa appeared in its full splendor. It wasn't as breathtaking as Istanbul, but it wasn't far from it. How could people be so wrong about their descriptions?

The landing, the unloading, and the registrations and paperwork that awaited us even before we stepped off the boat took several hours. Finally we walked on ground again, and as we were ready to enter a large hall a man in uniform came up to us and sprayed us with DDT. The smell was familiar since we had sometimes used DDT at home to kill bugs. It did not bother us at all. We smiled at the man and walked on eager to meet our Israeli family. Finally there they were: Tarzan, my mother's brother, and Efraim, Meir, and Isjue, my father's brothers. My Baba was not with them, and Tarzan explained to me in German that she could not travel that easily but she and Grandpa were fine and I would see them soon.

We sat together at a table in a little restaurant, and everybody was talking excitedly in German. At that moment I realized that I would never speak Romanian again and that a new era was beginning for me.

# Chapter Eighteen

# A New Beginning

The small and crowded bus left Haifa and continued on a narrow road to the kibbutz of two of my uncles, Mishmar Haemek. We were traveling through green hills and fields and very few houses. Suddenly I noticed brown tents in the middle of one of the fields. I asked my uncle what they were, and he explained that many refugees, like us, had come to Israel, and there wasn't enough housing for everybody so they had to live in tents. He added, "But you are coming with us, and you will stay with us on the kibbutz." I felt good: a new family, a new country, and now a kibbutz—the people I admired so much. I was very excited.

The bus entered a path with beautiful palm trees on both sides. My heart pounded in anticipation. Finally the bus stopped in an open area with a lot of beautiful lawns, trees, and flowers. It was midday; it was very hot, and the sun was beating on my head as I had never felt before. I saw people walking along the paths. They all wore shorts, hats, and sandals. They were tanned and healthy-looking. I suddenly felt out of place in my flowered dress and fancy shoes. I felt pallid and colorless next to them. I very much wanted to look like them.

We came to Mania and Meir's home. They had one small room with a porch on the second floor of a small building. Everything was neat and well-organized, and they also had a shower and toilet. I thought to myself, *How wonderful that they have their own shower in such a small apartment.* Everybody was very friendly and looked interested in us refugees, but I could only speak to my aunts and uncles since all my cousins spoke Hebrew, and I did not know Hebrew at all. Our first visit on the kibbutz was to my other grandmother, Sara, whom I had never met. She lived in a little house in a one-room apartment with neighbors her age. She was very different from my Baba, a small woman with a wig on her head and a long black dress. She was very excited and happy to see us and had all kinds of sweets ready for us. As we were sitting in her room a beautiful young girl walked in. She was introduced to us as Shifra, and she came over to me and spoke Yiddish to me. It turned out that she had survived the holocaust in Poland and was adopted by Froiku and Yadja (my other uncle and aunt at Mishmar Haemek). To me she looked like an ideal incarnation of a Sabra (although she was not born in Israel), and I was very happy to see that at least one young person could communicate with me. She looked so wonderful with her tanned skin and large beautiful blue eyes. She wore a *tembel* hat low on her forehead, shorts, and a sleeveless shirt. She sat down on the cool tile floor and looked seriously at us. I fell in love with her immediately.

As the evening came I was asked to come and sleep at Yadja and Froiku's place, and my parents stayed with Meir and Mania. We all slept on mattresses on the floor, and I wore my thin, embroidered nightgown, which we brought from Romania. This also felt out of place here where everybody wore shorts and cotton shirts. Still I was very excited and lay there for hours not being able to fall asleep. I was also very hot, not being used to the weather. Finally toward the morning I fell asleep, as the morning breeze blew gently through the shudders.

The next day Froike, who eventually turned out to be my favorite uncle, and who looked a lot like my father but was slower and gentler, took us all to see the kibbutz. We saw cows and sheep and hens, and I felt that I wanted to live here forever. Then they took us to the wonderful Mishmar Haemek forest. It was hot and dry but magical. The sound of the wind in the trees, the birds, the insects, the crackling of the pine needles—everything seemed so peaceful and beautiful. I did not then know that the beautiful forest would eventually become my place of retreat and the place where my father and I would have the most meaningful conversations in the following two years. What I did know was that I was drawn into the forest by a hidden magnet, and this added mystery and excitement to this new phase in my life.

After spending a few relaxed days on the kibbutz and just getting adjusted to the heat, the food, and the people, my parents began talking about finding work and an apartment in town. I wanted very much to see my Baba, but it was explained to me that the kibbutz was now in quarantine because of the mouth-and-hoof disease and I needed to stay there for a while. My parents had to leave, and they would only be able to come back about two weeks later. I accepted the situation and stayed with my uncle and aunt. Since they had to go to work every morning they decided to make a plan for me: in the morning I would go with Mania to work in the cowshed, then we would have lunch and we would come home to rest, in the afternoon a member of the kibbutz would come to teach me Hebrew, and then in the evening I would just spend time with the family. I was given a pair of shorts, a simple blouse, a hat, and a pair of sandals. Thus I could go to work everyday. Since I had to go to work with Mania I moved over to sleep at their house.

Early in the morning we woke up and without eating or drinking went to the cowshed. It was still dark outside, and the air was fresh and cooler. At the cowshed I was given a pair of heavy boots to wear and directions on how to do the cleaning. There were two other members of the kibbutz working there, and I could see that everybody respected Mania and followed her instructions. After about two hours, when the cows had been milked, the shed cleaned, and the food placed in front of the cows, we all sat down to breakfast. Tea and milk were brought from the cooler, and bread, cheese, and vegetables from the dining room. We sat on boxes and ate, and everybody was teaching me words in Hebrew. I was as happy as I could be. I didn't mind the smell or the dirt of the cowshed, I felt important and equal to everybody else.

Toward noon we went to take a shower in the communal shower for women. I was standing under the warm water and enjoying every drop. I had another pair of shorts and a blouse to put on after the shower that Mania gave me. So far I did not need my clothes from Romania. After the shower Mania took me to the dining hall. It was a small wooden shack, very crowded and noisy with many people in working outfits crowding around the table. Each person had a plate and a fork, but there was only one knife to be shared by all. A member came down the narrow aisle with a cart and put some food in everybody's plate. There were potatoes and a small meatball and some tomato. It all tasted very good. We ate fairly quickly and placed garbage into a metal bowl in the center of the table. I looked around and watched the people. Everybody seemed to know everybody else. Some smiled while talking to each other, others ate in silence—one big family. Every now and then someone came over to ask about me. They smiled at me, and only the older people said a word or two in German. I realized I had to learn the beautiful Hebrew language very fast, but somehow it was hard for me to remember the new words. The Russian words would pop up and interfere.

After lunch we went to rest. Everybody seemed to sleep for an hour or so. Meir came back from his work in the citrus orchards, and we all lay down. First I was too excited and could not sleep in the afternoon. Eventually I learned to close my eyes and nap for short periods of time, but I never really wanted to sleep. I wanted to go outside, see and do things.

Then Friday evening came. Everybody took showers in the afternoon and put on festive clothes: a white shirt and blue pants. I felt like dressing up too, so I took out my red skirt with beaded pockets and a light green blouse. I felt that these were the nicest clothes I had. That evening I was going to go for Friday night dinner with Yadja and Froiku. Shifra came over to the house, and she and Yadja were talking excitedly and looking at me. I did not know what they were saying, but Shifra looked at my clothes in disgust. Finally I asked Yadja what the matter was. She looked at me, smiled, and said: "Don't worry; it is nothing serious. Shifra does not think that you are dressed properly for the kibbutz, but I think you should not pay attention to this," and so we went to dinner in the dining hall. All that evening I looked at myself and at everybody else: Shifra was right, I was completely out of place. I would never wear this skirt or blouse again.

The following day was Saturday, and I walked again with Froiku through the kibbutz. I began to feel familiar and more at home. In the afternoon we all gathered at Mania's for four o'clock tea. Now I met my other cousins, Eddy, Yadja, and Froiku's only son, and Tamar and Hanan, Mania and Meir's children. Eddy was four years older than me, Tamar was seven years older than me, and Hanan was a little younger than me. I could see that Eddy and Tamar were interested in me and smiled at me often, but Hanan ignored me completely. I could not yet speak to any of them. Shifra sat down next to Tamar and talked to her about something. Then she said out loud, "What kind of a name is Melitta? It does not sound Hebrew at all, and Hadassah is not a name for a young girl. I suggest we call her Elite." I blushed, and my heart pounded wildly. I was just given a new name, a name that suited this new place, a name that would help me become part of this society. How exciting!

The following day Tamar met me in her parents' room. She was in her last month of pregnancy and was not working on a regular basis. She and her husband, Gideon, had been in the Israeli Defense Force during the War of Independence, and they had been taken prisoners by the Jordanian army. I had tremendous respect for her, and I was hoping to soon be able to speak to her. She showed me some clothes she brought for me: a few pairs of shorts and a beautifully embroidered white shirt. Later I learned that this was a Yemenite shirt and was considered the most beautiful attire a young girl could have. Mania explained that for a while Tamar would not be able to wear these clothes so I could have them for as long as I wished. Tamar also sat me down in front of her, combed my hair, and instead of the two braids that I was used to, she made a ponytail with my curly hair bunching up at the end of it. This was how she wore her hair as well, and both of us had very similar hair. I told myself that this was another step towards becoming a Sabra, which I was dying to be.

My Hebrew was improving rapidly, and I began to work in the laundry where Yadja used to work. I was quick to learn and eager to prove useful, and everybody liked me. Soon I got to know Uka, a friend of Mania's, and then I joined her at work tending the sheep. After two weeks my parents came to visit. They had found an apartment, and my father was going to start working in a building company. They seemed pleased and relaxed, and they looked at me in disbelief. "You look like a kibbutznik," my mother said.

My aunts and uncles and my parents talked about my future. The suggestion was made for me to stay on the kibbutz and go to the Mosad (the school on the kibbutz). My uncles convinced my parents that this was an excellent school, and I would be lucky to study there. So at the end of a long day of planning, my parents left and promised to come and visit two weeks later. I did not mind at all. I was learning new things about the kibbutz and its people, and so I was not really interested in going away with my parents.

Mania had just finished her term in the cowshed, and she was about to take on the kitchen. The new and very beautiful dining hall was being completed, and she began to organize the kitchen. She asked me if I would like to work with her in cleaning the new kitchen and make it ready for the inauguration of the new hall. I was delighted. This gave me an opportunity to meet new people and speak Hebrew all day long. I was so eager to prove myself that I worked for many hours every day, and everybody praised me for my work.

Two weeks passed, and my parents came again. This time they brought some paper from the Jewish agency promising payment to the kibbutz for my room and board at the school. They also brought me some new clothes, which they had bought with the money from the Jewish agency. My uncles said that now I needed to meet the principal of the school, and he would decide which class I was going to join. Soon after lunch, when everybody wanted to rest, my father and I decided to take a walk in the woods. This was the beginning of a long tradition we developed, walking in the woods on Saturday once every two weeks when they came to visit. On this first trip we discovered many quiet places and beautiful spots in the woods. We said that every Saturday we would take another path in order to get to know the various parts of the large forest. As we were walking my father would tell me about his youth and about Czernowitz, and I would tell him about things I had learned in the kibbutz. These were wonderful times of bonding and sharing.

One day my uncle Froiku took me to the principal of the school. He was a very tall and serious man who asked me a lot of questions in Hebrew. Then he gave me a little test in mathematics. Finally he said that he had two possibilities: I could join a class made up mostly of other immigrant children from different countries, but they were all a little older that me, or I could join a younger age group all made up of kibbutz children. I looked at my uncle, and I said, "I would like to be with kibbutz children."

The two men smiled at me, and the principal said, "Okay, you will be in the Shibolim group like your cousin, Hanan."

As we walked back from the principal I realized that I had to make a big decision: *From now on my Romanian is dead. I will never speak it again. Everything I have done so far is not important—I must behave and live like a Sabra. I want to become as similar as possible to*

***Shifra and Tamar.*** The following Saturday I took my diary, which was written in Romanian, my last book from Romania that I had read (*40 days on the Musah Dag*), and my red skirt with the beaded pockets, and I went to the forest by myself. There I dug a little hole in the ground, buried all these things, and lit a little fire on top. I sat in front of the small bonfire and felt that I was disconnecting myself from the past. I was careful to extinguish the fire and cover it all up with a lot of dirt, and then I walked back to the kibbutz feeling light and free.

# Chapter Nineteen

# Becoming a Sabra

Finally one Saturday when my parents came to visit, I was told that I could go and visit them in Haifa and also go and visit my grandmother on the other kibbutz, Maabarot. At the end of the Sabbath visit, I packed my things and joined my parents on the bus to Haifa. I had two weeks before school started, and I wanted to see as much of Israel as I could in these two weeks.

My parents were living in one room of a four-room apartment with other three families who lived in the other rooms and a large hall shared by all. They shared the porch with one of the families and the kitchen with another. The bathroom and toilet were shared by all four families, so one had to make a lot of adjustments. The apartment was on the fourth floor of a tall, Arab building, and from our porch and windows one could see the beautiful Mount Carmel. On the first night, I sat on the porch and watched the lights of Haifa. It was so beautiful, like a lit up Christmas tree, and I could not go to sleep.

The next morning the happy moment finally arrived, and my Baba came to visit us. I had not seen her for over two years, and I was so pleased to see that she looked well and seemed happy. My father had gone to work early in the morning. and my mother explained to me that she and Baba had a very important job to do: They were going to look for some diamonds, which had been hidden in two down pillows that we brought with us from Romania. She tried to find them herself, but it was an impossible job since they had been sewn into pieces of white cotton, and now it was necessary to carefully check every piece of white down, hoping to find the tiny and very expensive stones. If I had the patience, I could join them.

We made some sandwiches in the kitchen, staying carefully within our corner, and then locked ourselves in our room. First we opened one pillow and sat down on the floor with the down spread all around us. We carefully fingered every piece, and then put it back in the pillowcase. Finally after hours of search my grandmother found the first diamond, and I found the second toward the evening of a long and tiring day. My mother was exhausted but very happy. She said that selling these two diamonds would make it possible for them to rent a place where they could start their own marble business again. Within a few weeks the plan was realized, and my parents began to activate their own business in the bay area of Haifa.

As for myself, I was dying to go back to the kibbutz, but first I had to visit my Baba in her kibbutz and see how my grandfather Leizer was doing. They were living in a small house near the beautiful dining room in Kibbutz Maabarot. This was a very central location, and Baba was very pleased. My grandfather, like always, slept most of the day and just got up to eat something or take a few steps in the small room. Sometimes he sat in a chair in front of the house and looked at the people passing by.

My uncle Tarzan and his wife, Zipora, were kind and considerate and visited my grandparents daily on their way to the dining hall. They always brought them nice things to eat and stayed and talked to them in German. There were many other members of Maabarot who knew my grandparents from Czernowitz and who stopped to talk to them. I looked at my beloved grandparents, and I thought to myself, *Finally they have a good life, and they can enjoy their old age*. They also had three wonderful grandsons on the kibbutz, but they could not speak to them since my grandparents did not know Hebrew.

I stayed with Baba for a whole week. I told her everything about our trip to Israel and about the other kibbutz. She was happy to hear every detail of my stories. "I am very lucky to have lived to see your family together again, your father and your mother. Who could believe what we have been through. And now, all of you are well and happy here in Palestine. I have just one wish—to live to dance on your wedding." We both laughed at that and hugged each other happily.

On the last day before I left my grandparents to return to my kibbutz and begin the new school year, Baba sat me down near her in front of the large window of her little house. She said to me, "Littika, you know, I sit here everyday and look at the beautiful girls who pass by. And there are some truly beautiful girls on the kibbutz, but none, not even one, is half as beautiful as you are. I am so happy to see how you have grown to be a lovely young girl. I hope your luck in life will be just as good." I listened to her, and I knew she was exaggerating and trying to please me and make me happy, but it was a wonderful feeling to know that this was what she thought of me. During hard times and trying moments I remembered her words, and that always brought a smile to my lips.

After the long summer I went back to Mishmar Haemek. This was a new beginning. Now was my opportunity to become a Sabra, to prove that I could be like everyone else on the kibbutz. This time I felt like this was my own choice, and it would depend on me alone how well I integrated.

As I arrived at the Mosad, the kibbutz school situated on the top of a hill, I met our instructor, Dina, who was a nice and friendly woman in charge of our age group. She showed me to my room, which I shared with three other youngsters, one girl and two boys. She explained to me that on the kibbutz boys and girls slept together like family. The girls had the beds on one side of the room and the boys on the other. We were not supposed to be shy about sharing a room, and we were also expected to use common showers. I had heard about it before coming to the school, but now I was truly worried. *I am very shy even around girl;s how can I sleep in the same room with boys and shower in the same shower room?*

Dina looked at me and seemed to understand. She said, "You will get used to it, don't worry, but when you have your period, you will use the shower of the 'bashful girls.'" I realized that the "bashful girls' shower" was for those who had their period, but also for those who were simply "bashful" so I felt that there was an escape exit from this situation.

Near my bed I had a closet and room for personal items. I put my few things there and walked around the building. More youngsters were coming with their things and were assigned rooms. Among the kibbutz children there were two or three urban children who stood out because of their uneasy behavior. I felt like them, but I decided not to make friends until I saw who my classmates were. In the late afternoon Dina got us all together in a classroom, which was on the same floor as our bedrooms. She welcomed us all, and she explained the routine of our life. At six o'clock every morning the sound of a bugle would wake us up. At six thirty we were to go to the sports arena and participate in morning exercises (which I knew my beautiful cousin Shifra was leading). At seven we ate breakfast, and at eight we should be in our classroom ready to begin the school day. Before going to the classroom we should make our beds and leave the rooms in an orderly fashion. There was a break in the middle of the morning when we got fresh fruit to eat, and at noon we all went for lunch. Then there was time to rest till two o'clock when we each reported for work to our assigned areas. Each quarter, each student would work in a different section and field of work. She gave each person the assignment for the school year: my first term was in the corn fields, my second term in the kitchen, and my third term tending the sheep in the children's farm. I understood most of what she said in Hebrew, and I began to look around to consider who my future friends would be. When Dina introduced me she said, "Elite is a refugee from Romania, but she is not in the immigrant class. She will be one of your group, and you should help her become a Sabra." Some of the boys looked suspiciously at me, and the girls ignored me. Later I understood that my status in this society was very low: I was not a kibbutznik (but an "outsider" in the local language), and I was not a Sabra." If they could help it, they would not have anything to do with me. But I did not care. I knew that I was going to make it eventually, and as Baba always said, "Do what you have to do with love and care, even if it feels terrible."

In the afternoon after we finished our work in the respective areas, we were free until the evening meal. This was the time to visit parents for the kibbutz children and for me to visit my aunts and uncles, Froiku and Yadja and Meir and Mania. They were always happy to see me, and I enjoyed their "four o'clock tea," which reminded me of our *yause* in Czernowitz.

Joining the group at school automatically made me a candidate for becoming a Shomer Hatzair member. A few weeks after school started we had a big ceremony in a sports field. The big slogans were written in fire, and we were put in rows at attention. The Shomer Hatzair instructor read all the names of the newcomers, and we became members. I had my blue blouse with white laces, and I was very proud. Twice a week, we had Shomer Hatzair meetings, which sometimes reminded me of my days in the Russian pioneers because they talked about the meaning of socialism and communism. Other times we had intense group discussions dealing with relations among ourselves. On holidays we had special events in Shomer Hatzair, and these were times of personal elation for me. We used to stand in our groups like scouts—the big signs and slogans were lit up, and we listened to speeches and sang songs. I always felt like finally I was part of my people, of a group of young and beautiful Israelis who were honest, hard-working, and very intelligent. I felt very fortunate to be part of this new beginning, a new beginning for me personally, as well.

The first year at the Mosad school was hard, exciting and intense. I woke up every morning before the bugle so that I could put on my clothes before the boys got up. I went to shower at times when there were fewer kids in the shower, and I pretended not to see anyone. I made friends with the girl in my room, who was a very weak student and not very well-liked by others, but for me she was a connection to the locals, and I made friends with another girl who was an outsider. I also made friends with some of the boys who worked with me in the cornfields. I fulfilled all my duties religiously. I was the fastest worker in the fields in the first term of the year, I cleaned the kitchen perfectly the second term, and I enjoyed milking the sheep early in the morning and taking them out to pasture in the afternoon in the third term. I continued going to the woods with my father every second Saturday when my parents came to visit. My Hebrew improved very fast, and I also began learning English. I soon excelled in English and moved from the lowest level to the highest level and could help other students in their work. I felt that my social position was getting stronger, and soon some of the kibbutz girls began to show more interest in me. Toward the end of the year I felt that I had basically made it into this new society of kids, and I was happy and proud of myself. When I visited Baba during vacation times I always told her about my friends and my work at the Mosad school. We used to walk hand in hand to the dining hall, and I felt that my Baba was proud and happy. She often said, "I have just one wish in my heart; I want to live long enough to be at your wedding."

When the summer vacation came, I went to stay with my parents for a while and of course visit Baba at Maabarot. In the middle of the summer vacation I was supposed to return to Mishmar Haemek in order to join my group for a Shomer Hatzair summer camp. Although I had been told the date and exact time when I was supposed to arrive ready to go on the trip, when I got off the bus from Haifa I discovered to my dismay that they had left two hours earlier than planned and they had forgotten all about me. I was terribly disappointed, and I tried to consult Mania on what to do, but she said, "I don't think you can do anything. They all left by bus early in the morning, and they are in a forest several hours from here. We cannot get in touch with them, and I don't see what you can do. Just stay with us and have a nice vacation." I felt tears chocking me, and I did not want to give up.

I was sitting like this, upset and sad in front of the dining hall, when a young member of the kibbutz came by and stopped to talk to me. I had worked with her, and she liked me. When I told her the story she said, "You know what, you can still make it. Go up to the road and catch a ride to the town of Afula. There go to the bus station and take a bus to Kibbutz Beth Alfa. Get off at the gate and ask someone how to walk to the forest where the Shomer Hatzair camp is. It cannot be more than an hour's walk and you will be there. The whole thing should not take you more than three or four hours, so you can join them still before it gets dark." I listened to her very attentively and a new hope kindled in my heart. I was thirteen years old, quite adventurous and sure of myself, I felt strong and independent, and I was going to do it. I told Mania of my plan. She made me two nice sandwiches and gave me some money for the bus, and I was on my way.

On the road a small jeep with two men stopped for me. I got in and was a little worried but they brought me safely to the bus station in Afula. There were many people at the bus stations speaking many different languages. I found the bus to Beth Alfa and was lucky to get on it at noon. An hour later I was waking on the road from Beth Alfa to the forest, munching on the sandwiches that Mania gave me. The sun was hot and the road quite deserted, but I enjoyed both the sandwiches and the freedom and independence of my actions. Soon I reached some woods, and I could hear sounds and voices of youngsters. I walked straight into a very large camp with groups of Shomer Hatzair people from all over the country. I asked for the Mishmar Haemek group, and I was directed to their part of the camp. Slowly I walked into the camp, some of my friends suddenly realized that I was there, and they all surrounded me. They could not believe that I had done this trip all by myself, and they were very impressed. I was the hero of the day, and I felt great. Was I now fully accepted by them? I would have to do well on this camp before I could feel like a Sabra.

The various camps had a competition for the cleanest, most beautiful site. We had to whitewash the stones surrounding the tents and clean the paths leading to the tents, making the eating area look neat and beautiful. I volunteered to be in charge. I had never worked so hard before, but in the end our group won the prize. All the kids cheered for me and praised me. On the bus, going back to the kibbutz with the whole group, I finally felt that I was one of them. My second year on the kibbutz would be a pleasure.

# Epilogue

I am now a retired professor of language education from Hebrew University living in Jerusalem, Israel. I have had a wonderful career—specializing in the teaching of English as a second language. I have a wonderful family, a loving husband, Zeev, three beautiful and successful daughters married to three kind and loving young men, and so far nine grandchildren, four boys and five girls. This book was something I felt I had to do in order to connect my childhood to the new generations and to say out loud what many Holocaust survivors often say: "Hitler wanted to exterminate our people, and our best revenge is the fact that we managed to raise a new family in a new country in spite of the suffering that was inflicted upon us as children."

After a few years on the kibbutz school I joined my parents, who had moved to Ramat Gan, a small town near Tel Aviv. I studied at a high school in Ramat Gan and became an excellent student, winning a scholarship that paid for my tuition. I was very strong in English, so I had the possibility to teach younger children and thus earn money from the age of fifteen. I made enough money to buy my school uniforms, my books, and all my personal necessities without having to burden my parents, who worked very hard to build a new life for themselves.

I began my academic studies as a student of economics, a year before I was recruited to the Israeli Defence Army. During the army service I continued my studies in the evening, and a year after my army service I received my first degree. At the university I met my husband, Zeev, and we got married in 1959 when I was twenty-one and a half years old. My grandmother Sabina, who was eighty years old, came to my wedding and beamed with happiness. She had a stroke while we were on our honeymoon, and she passed away a few months later. She always wanted to make it to my wedding, and she lived to do so.

After getting married, Zeev and I studied at UCLA in the US. We lived in Los Angeles for various periods of time. I received my MA, gave birth to my first daughter, Tali, and finally received my PhD in the States. I am today fully bilingual in Hebrew and English and feel equally comfortable in both languages and both cultures. I still understand German perfectly but speak a bit haltingly since now I have very little opportunity to practice the language. I forgot Romanian completely and stopped using the language from the day I arrived in Israel.

My parents, Willy and Frieda, reached old age with Frieda passing away at the age of eighty-nine in 2001 and my father at the age of ninety-five in 2003. Frieda went to her marble workshop, which had long stopped functioning, till the last day of her life.

During my parents' life I did not have the courage to begin to write this book. After they passed away, I began various investigations into the events that took place during my childhood. My youngest daughter, Orly, helped me do the research, and my husband, Zeev, supplied me with support and encouragement. My daughters Tali and Karen read my writing critically and offered the vision leading to the final version. This was definitely a family venture.

Finally in the summer of 2006 I visited Czernowitz and Murafa, together with Zeev. My good friend Bella acted as our interpreter and guide. We drove into Czernowitz late at night. My heart was pounding and my eyes were humid, but I could not recognize anything. When we walked out into the street the next morning I looked around, but the people spoke only Ukrainian. Nobody spoke German, and no one looked familiar. Then our tour guide arrived with a map. I pointed out the street on which I was born and which I knew from my old German map to be Franzensgasse. Now it was called "The 28$^{th}$ of June," the date when the Russians entered the city the first time. I could not remember the number of the house.

We went to our street. It began to look familiar, but I was still quite confused. I told the guide that my parents were married in 1935 and they moved into an apartment in a new building. She smiled and said, "I will take you to your house since in 1935 they built only *bau* house style, and there is just one such building on this street." I stepped out of the car, and there was the building I remembered from my childhood. We walked into the staircase, and I stopped on the spot where my mother met me when she returned from Transnistria. Then we knocked on the door, and the woman living there now let us in. The furniture was unfamiliar, but everything else was just the way I remembered it, even the terracotta ovens were there, exactly as sixty years earlier, although they were not being used for heating anymore.

From the apartment we walked to the Ring Platz, the same stretch I often used to walk with my grandmother. Now I recognized many buildings and of course the Herren Gasse. Our guide took us to Rosh, and I remembered meeting my father there. Then we went to the Jewish cemetery, and our excitement reached its height when we found my father's signature on some of the granite tomb stones. We ended up in the beautiful train station from where my mother was taken to Transnistria. Everything looked calm, and it was impossible to imagine the people being hurdled onto the trains in 1941. I wanted to know whether we could take the train to Moghilev, but they told us that there were no trains in that direction.

We decided to drive by ourselves to Murafa. This was the little village in which my mother had spent two and a half difficult years. The roads were bad and the directions unclear. Finally after asking many farmers on the road, we reached Murafa. Bella approached some women on the road and asked for the oldest people in town who could tell us something about the time of the war. One of the women took us to the "oldest" man who lived in a tiny house with a neglected backyard. He and his wife, who could barely walk, told us that they remembered the Jews who lived in the village during the war. "They had to work hard," the old man said, "but the stronger ones survived the typhus and the lack of food. They were not killed in Murafa, but they were deported beyond the Bug." We wanted to see the hospital where Frieda had worked, but the hospital does not exist today. It was there at the time to serve the German army. The old man remembered a young woman named Frieda who worked there.

When we visited the Ukraine most of the book had been written. There was very little that needed adjustment. My memories seemed to be quite true to life. This was a true story as seen through the eyes of a little girl.